The Ancient Church:
And our Fundamental Beliefs

Dec 18

ED,
IT'S BEEN great
Having you IN class.
Always FUN!
Thank you
Kristy Seiber

20/20
BIBLE
PUBLICATIONS
Acts 20:20

(copied from a Bible circa 1500)

The Apostles Crossing the Sea of Galilee (Mark 4:35-40)

The Ancient Church:
And our Fundamental Beliefs

Keith M. Seiber

20/20 Bible Publications
2018

First Printing: 2018

All Bible quotations are taken from the King James Version of the Bible.

All pictures used in this publication are in the public domain or used by permission. PD-ART (PD-old-100), PD-old-1923, PD-ART (PD-old-auto-1923) – See Contents for page number for specific picture credits. At the time of this publication, all efforts had been made to determine proper credit. Please contact 20/20 Bible Publications if any are inaccurate.

ISBN 978-0-359-17231-3

20/20 Bible Publications
11281 W Ruddy Drive
Marana, AZ 85653

www.2020bible.pub

Order more copies from:

http://www.lulu.com/spotlight/2020bibleclub or 2020bible.pub

Other books available for 20/20 Bible Publications:

Wisdoms Path
Giving… "unto the furtherance of the Gospel"
Bible Character Volume 1
Yes… It Does Matter
Peace in the Storm
The Life of Christ
Cold Christians
Islam & the Christian
Homosexuality, Marriage & the Bible
How will you be Judged?
Note Takers & Quiet Time Journal
What does the Bible say about Cutting?

Contents

Introduction

When you begin reading this book you will embark on a trip through our early church history. We will begin with where it all started with Jesus and the Apostles and the start of the church. This book will hop around to examine the lives of the Apostles, and the very Ancient church immediately after the lives of the Apostles.

I hope you are ready to begin the adventure and awe inspiring journey ahead as you begin your reading I encourage you to try to place yourself in the setting's you will read about, try to envision with your mind's eye what is going on in the situations we will examine and ask yourself: would I be so noble, would I be so true, or would I stand so firm on Christ and His Word?

Mentioned often in this book is the term "Fundamental DNA"; this is a term I use to describe or refer to the most basic and purest form of our Christian beliefs and practice. The closer we are to being a pure and truly fundamental people in our faith and practice, the closer we are to the New Testament standard.

DNA is the basic information content of an organism. The church is a living organism of its own kind. Encoded in DNA are 3.1 billion letters of information, that basically are the program of the cell. Encoded into every church should be God's Word as the guiding program or document of all faith and practice. When DNA starts to mutate, when DNA starts to get corrupted, when it has other things added to it, or has part of it taken away, the organism whose DNA this is happening to does not function properly, does not act properly, does not look like it should; because the DNA has become perverted, it has become polluted and it is no longer, in many cases, able to do what it was originally designed to do.

I believe this makes an excellent parallel to describe the living organism of the church. We should desire to be pure, we should desire to look, to act, and to function as the church was originally designed and intended to do. My point is some churches still are functioning as originally designed, their DNA is not corrupted, nor has it been changed, or added to or taken from, and those churches are the ones that adhere to all the basic fundamentals of the faith. It should be the goal of all Christians and all churches to have this pure Fundamental DNA at their core, uncorrupted, unchanged and pure by the Word of God.

At the end of each chapter will be a section highlighting a few key fundamental principles that can be gleaned from the histories and teachings of each chapter to demonstrate that fundamental DNA present all throughout church history.

THE FOUNDING OF THE CHURCH

Ephesians 5:25 *"...Christ also loved the church, and gave himself for it;"*

In Bible study there are various laws, rules, and methods of study. One of the methods is the Law of First Mention. We are going to begin this study on church history, on where we should begin it, at the founding of the church itself. We are going to look at the first two times "church" is used in the New Testament. This will be the very first building block, the foundation, the backbone, the spiral staircase looking structure if you will, that our fundamental church DNA is built upon and attached to. So we need to first examine this base structure, this foundation of the true church before we delve into further examination of the church itself. We are going to look carefully at the first two mentions of the foundation of the church and of our Fundamental beliefs.

WHEN DID THE CHURCH BEGIN?

Matthew 16:13-19 *"When Jesus came into the coasts of Caesarea Philippi, he asked his disciples, saying, Whom do men say that I the Son of man am? And they said, Some say that thou art John the Baptist: some, Elias; and others, Jeremias, or one of the prophets. He saith unto them, But whom say ye that I am? And Simon Peter answered and said, Thou art the Christ, the Son of the living God. And Jesus answered and said unto him, Blessed art thou, Simon Barjona: for flesh and blood hath not revealed it unto thee, but my Father which is in heaven. And I say also unto thee, That thou art Peter, and upon this rock **I will build my church**; and the gates of hell shall not prevail against it."*

Our next occurrence of the word church in the New Testament is found in Matthew chapter 18. The word church is found in the New Testament some 113 times.

Matthew 18:15-19 *"Moreover if thy brother shall trespass against thee, go and tell him his fault between thee and him alone: if he shall hear thee, thou hast gained thy brother. But if he will not hear thee, then take with thee one or two more, that in the mouth of two or three witnesses every word may be established. And if he shall neglect to hear them, tell it unto **the church**: but if he neglect to hear the church, let him be unto thee as an heathen man and a publican."*

Look at the two expressions isolated in *Matthew 16:18* "*I WILL BUILD MY CHURCH*" and *Matthew 18:17* "*TELL IT TO THE CHURCH*". These are the first two mentions of the word "church" in the New Testament and in the Bible. There is no such thing as the church as we know, with two ordinances, church officers, a Great Commission to fulfill, mentioned in the Old Testament. We can find some pictures of the church in the Old Testament, such as Eve being the bride of Adam and Sarah being the bride of Abraham. The Old Testament teaching is primarily not on the church.

So when did the church begin? We know by the reading Matthew 16 Jesus said, "*I will build my church.*" So the church was apparently yet future when Jesus spoke those words. Not long after speaking these words Jesus died on the cross and rose the third day. Pentecost came, and all the component parts of the church were in place. So think for a moment. What does the Bible say the church is founded upon? What makes up the double helix of our fundamental church DNA? The Bible teaches us that the church is founded upon the death, the resurrection, and the ascension of Christ.

"Ascension of Christ"

Gustave Dore (1832-1883)

The Bible teaches us that Jesus intercedes for the church in Heaven. How can He intercede there, if He is not there? Also, the Bible teaches us that when Jesus ascended on high, that He led captivity captive, He moved the saints from Abrahams bosom and took them to Heaven with Him. So Christians became part of one body, the church on the day of Pentecost. One more point on this topic, the Holy Spirit never inhabited believers, as He does today, until the day of Pentecost, now look at what *Ephesians 2:21-22* says *"In whom all the building fitly framed together groweth unto an holy temple in the Lord: In whom ye also are builded together for an habitation of God through the Spirit."*

Acts 2:1-7 *"And when the day of Pentecost was fully come, they were all with one accord in one place. And suddenly there came a sound from heaven as of a rushing mighty wind, and it filled all the house where they were sitting. And there appeared unto them cloven tongues like as of fire, and it sat upon each of them. And they were all filled with the Holy Ghost, and began to speak with other tongues, as the Spirit gave them utterance. And there were dwelling at Jerusalem Jews, devout men, out of every nation under heaven. Now when this was noised abroad, the multitude came together, and were confounded, because that every man heard them speak in his own language. And they were all amazed and marvelled, saying one to another, Behold, are not all these which speak Galilaeans?"*

"Pentecost" (1550)

Giulio Clovio (1498-1578)

ON WHO IS THE CHURCH FOUNDED?

Who is the church founded upon? You may think this is a question all Christians should know the answer to. It may seem to you to be a simple question with a simple answer. But the truth is, there are many people who claim to be Christians out there who do not know for sure the answer to the question, and there are many who think they do know the answer, except it is the wrong answer that they know. For instance, Catholics will say and teach that Jesus founded His church upon the Apostle Peter based on their reading and understanding of *Matthew 16*. Getting this answer correct is fundamental to who we are and to our faith and practice. The answer to this question is foundational to the fundamental DNA of the church. Millions of people around the world do not believe the church is founded upon Jesus Christ. So this section may seem simple to some, but we have to get this part right, to have the solid foundation to build our lives and the church upon.

The Lord gave us a great illustration to understand this point in ***Matthew 7:24-27*** *"Therefore whosoever heareth these sayings of mine, and doeth them, I will liken him unto a wise man, which built his house upon a rock: And the rain descended, and the floods came, and the winds blew, and beat upon that house; and it fell not: for it was founded upon a rock. And every one that heareth these sayings of mine, and doeth them not, shall be likened unto a foolish man, which built his house upon the sand: And the rain descended, and the floods came, and the winds blew, and beat upon that house; and it fell: and great was the fall of it."*

Now, while thinking about this illustration in Matthew chapter 7, let's look again at what Jesus says in *Matthew 16:18* *"upon this rock I will build my church"*. So the church was founded upon an unmovable, large, strong rock suitable for an eternal foundation, not a small pebble, not something that could be picked up and thrown, but a solid, permanent, stable, eternally secure rock. Now with this thought in mind, the rest of *Matthew 16:18* makes sense *"and the gates of hell shall not prevail against it."*

As mentioned earlier, some people and churches will say that Peter was that rock Jesus was referencing building His church upon. One way they get this thinking and this belief from is *John 1:42* *"And he brought him to Jesus. And when Jesus beheld him, he said, Thou art Simon the son of Jona: thou shalt be called Cephas, which is by interpretation, A stone."* Now let's look at *Matthew 16:17-20* *"And Jesus answered and said unto him, Blessed art thou, Simon Barjona: for flesh and blood hath not revealed it unto thee, but my Father which is in heaven. And I say also unto thee, That thou art Peter, and upon this rock I will build my church; and the gates of hell shall not prevail against it. And I will give unto thee the keys of the kingdom of heaven: and whatsoever thou shalt bind on earth shall be bound in heaven: and whatsoever thou shalt loose on earth shall be loosed in heaven. Then charged he his disciples that they should tell no man that he was Jesus the Christ."*

The following comment on this passage from *The Wiersbe Bible Commentary* sums up the issue:

These Jewish men, steeped in Old Testament Scripture, recognized the rock as a symbol of God. "He is the Rock; his work is perfect" (Deut. 32:4). "The Lord is my rock, and my fortress" (Ps. 18:2). "For who is God save the Lord? Or who is a rock save our God?" (Ps. 18:31).

But let's investigate the Greek words that the Holy Spirit led Matthew to use. "Thou art petros [a stone], and upon this rock [petra—a large rock] I will build my church." Jesus had given Simon the new name of Peter (John 1:42) which means "a stone." The Aramaic form is Cephas, which also means "a stone." Everyone who believes in Jesus Christ and confesses Him as the Son and God and Savior, are "lively stones" (1 Peter 2:5).

Jesus Christ is the foundation rock on which the church is built. The Old Testament prophets said so (Ps. 118:22; Isa. 28:16). Jesus Himself said this (Matt. 21:42) and so did Peter and the other apostles (Acts 4:10–12). Paul also stated that the foundation for the church is Jesus Christ (1 Cor. 3:11). This foundation was laid by the apostles and prophets as they preached Christ to the lost (1 Cor. 2:1–2; 3:11; Eph. 2:20).

In other words, when the evidence is examined, the total teaching of Scripture is that the church, God's temple (Eph. 2:19–22), is built on Jesus Christ—not on Peter. How could God build His church on a fallible man like Peter? Later, the same Peter who

confessed Christ became an adversary and enter-
tained Satan's thoughts (Matt. 16:22ff.). "But that
was before Peter was filled with the Spirit," some ar-
gue. Then consider Peter's doctrinal blunders
recorded in Galatians 2, blunders that had to be dealt
with by Paul. This event occurred after Peter was
filled with the Spirit. [1]

I Corinthians 3:11 *"For other foundation can no man lay than that
is laid, which is Jesus Christ."*

Albert Barnes, in his New Testament Commentary, made the following comment of Christ being the foundation of the church *"Christ
is often called the foundation; the stone; the corner stone on which
the church is reared, Isa 28:16; Mt 21:42; Ac 4:11; Eph 2:20; 2Ti
2:19; 1Pe 2:6. The meaning is, that no true church can be reared
which does not embrace and hold the true doctrines respecting him-
-those which pertain to his incarnation, his Divine nature, his in-
structions, his example, his atonement, his resurrection, and his
ascension. The reason why no true church can be established without embracing the truth as it is in Christ, is, that it is by him only that
men can be saved; and where this doctrine is wanting, all is wanting
that enters into the essential idea of a church. The fundamental doctrines of the Christian religion must be embraced, or a church
cannot exist; and where those doctrines are denied, no association
of men can be recognized as a church of God. Nor can the foundation
be modified or shaped so as to suit the wishes of men. It must be laid*

---

[1] Wiersbe, W. (2007). *The Wiersbe Bible Commentary.* Colorado Springs, CO: David C.
Cook.k

as it is in the Scriptures; and the superstructure must be reared on that alone."

Phillip Doddridge also had a great comment of Christ being the foundation of the church and our faith – *"This is all indeed that remains to be done; for other solid foundation no one is able to lay beside what is already laid, which is Jesus Christ, the great foundation-stone which God hath laid in Zion, elect and precious; and I take it for granted, no one who calls himself a Christian will attempt to lay any other."* Phillip Doddrige was a preacher of the Gospel in England until his death in 1751. He declined becoming part of the church of England, and instead became an independent Pastor leading an independent congregation separate from the church of England. He did this because he felt there should be no earthly hierarchy over the church and that only One should have the preeminence over the local church and that was Christ and Christ alone. (*Colossians 1:15-19 - Who is the image of the invisible God, the firstborn of every creature: For by him were all things created, that are in heaven, and that are in earth, visible and invisible, whether they be thrones, or dominions, or principalities, or powers: all things were created by him, and for him: And he is before all things, and by him all things consist. And he is the head of the body, the church: who is the beginning, the firstborn from the dead; that in all things he might have the preeminence. For it pleased the Father that in him should all fulness dwell;*)

THE ESSENTIALS OF THE CHURCH

(Matthew 16:13-19)

In this passage in *Matthew 16*, Christ focused on the essentials of the church. The essentials to a car are the engine, transmission, brakes and electrical system. If you do not have these basic essentials of a car, having just a steering wheel and some tires, do not get you anywhere. Christ spoke the words in our passage of study to men He took time to disciple. So discipling is definitely an essential of the church, Christ also commands as much in *Matthew 28:18-20*. Christ told Peter that the only reason he stated the correct answer to His question was because the Father illuminated his mind to the right answer. Christ must always be the head of the church, as He is the one that founded it and is the foundation of it (*Ephesians 1:22-23*). Another essential of the church is the involvement of the Holy Spirit; He must be in the midst of the church, He must be inhabiting the Christians in the church, because you have to be saved to be part of the church. The Holy Spirit does the work of illuminating the Word, which is another essential of the church, to those who are saved, salvation of one's soul is an essential aspect of one being part of the church.

The number one essential of the church is Christ. Unless Christ is the center of everything in the church, there is no point in doing anything. It can be compared to a person believing in Christ for salvation, but not believing in the resurrection or life after death, what is the point then? Not having Christ in the center of all the church does, is like being alive but choosing not to have a heart or lungs. You won't be alive very long without them and a church that neglects to put Christ in the center of all it does won't be alive very long either.

Christ must be everything He says He is or He is not Christ at all (*I John 4:4 - Ye are of God, little children, and have overcome them: because greater is he that is in you, than he that is in the world.*) Reading the Bible while practicing what it says is essential, loving others while serving them, so they can come to know Christ and be more like Him, is essential.

The church is the only place that Christ is the head of and the place He is directly attached (*Ephesians 1:22-23 - And hath put all things under his feet, and gave him to be the head over all things to the church, Which is his body, the fulness of him that filleth all in all.*) It is a place to call the elders together to pray for healing (*James 5:14-16*). It is the place you discover your spiritual gifts and use them to serve others and minister to a hurt and broken world. It is the place the Pastor can be found to help minister to broken lives. It is the place where Christ wants His death to be remembered (*I Corinthians 11:24-26*). The church is the pillar and foundation of truth. The building of the church is where the family of God gathers each week and it is where love matters most (*I John 4:8 - He that loveth not knoweth not God; for God is love.*)

> *H.W. Beecher* says that "*some churches are like lighthouses, built of stone, so strong that the thunder of the sea cannot move them...*" The light that shines from these churches is the light of Christ shining through His believers. Sinners are not reached solely

through the church's ceremony, pomp, beautiful music or largeness – they are reached through the Christ-likeness of its individual members. [2]

Christ and His Word is the foundation that all our fundamental beliefs are built upon. We need the church as established by Christ to add all the component parts of what has become known as our Independent Baptist churches of today. The church is the basis of everything, without it we have nothing to build upon. The foundation of the church is Jesus Christ. He is the head of the church, the founder of the church, the interceder for the church, and the Savior of the church. Everything centers on Christ, as should everything in our life too.

Chapter One Key Fundamental Principles:

1.) Key Fundamental - **Christ is the foundation of the church**. He is the head of the church. He is who founded the church, started the church and continues to intercede on behalf of the church to this day. There are those all around us that do not have Christ as the foundation of their life, have you told them about Jesus?

2.) Key Fundamental – **Discipleship**. From the very beginning discipleship was not only a command and an essential component of the church, it was also necessary for the proper functioning of the church. Discipleship is how we pass on our fundamental beliefs and practices, it is how we can help train and equip young believers in Christ to go out, and in

---

[2] Steele, R. (1995). *Practical Bible Illustrations from Yesterday and Today.* Chattanooga, TN: AMG International, Inc.

turn win others and perpetuate the process from generation to generation. Ask yourself: "Am I doing my part to help disciple others like I should be?

THE APOSTLES – Part 1

Matthew 28:18-20 - And Jesus came and spake unto them, saying, All power is given unto me in heaven and in earth. Go ye therefore, and teach all nations, baptizing them in the name of the Father, and of the Son, and of the Holy Ghost: Teaching them to observe all things whatsoever I have commanded you: and, lo, I am with you alway, even unto the end of the world. Amen.

Jesus commissioned his Apostles at the end of his earthly ministry to carry on his work until He comes back. This commission not only applied to his disciples, it applies to all of us today as well. We are all commanded, and expected to fulfill this Great Commission. A key fundamental doctrine is that of fulfilling the Great Commission with zeal and fervency. We can see where that key fundamental doctrine of strong aggressive evangelism came from, where the DNA of that fundamental characteristic originated; and that was from Christ Himself and the example that was set by the Apostles.

"FOR TO ME TO LIVE IS CHRIST AND TO DIE IS GAIN" - *Philippians 1:21*

The Apostles, after the close of the Gospel and New Testament records of their life, did not then live happily ever after. The Christian Church was in its infancy and was heavily and severely persecuted during the first few centuries after the death of Christ.

John the Baptist, was the first in a long line of martyrs over the centuries for Christ. Those whose only crime was being a Christian were then put to death because of that belief. These martyrs gave their whole life over to Christ, they laid their all on the alter for Him. Following their Savior, in sometimes rapid succession, many other martyred heroes died. The next one to mention is Stephen. He was one of the first Deacons. He was also a preacher of the Gospel of Christ. His death is recorded for us in Acts chapters 7 and 8. His death is important to mention in our study of the Apostles because a future Apostle was there at the stoning of Stephen consenting to the death of Stephen. (*Acts 7:54-8:1 - When they heard these things, they were cut to the heart, and they gnashed on him with their teeth. But he, being full of the Holy Ghost, looked up stedfastly into heaven, and saw the glory of God, and Jesus standing on the right hand of God, And said, Behold, I see the heavens opened, and the Son of man standing on the right hand of God. Then they cried out with a loud voice, and stopped their ears, and ran upon him with one accord, And cast him out of the city, and stoned him: and the witnesses laid down their clothes at a <u>young man's feet, whose name was Saul.</u> And they stoned Stephen, calling upon God, and saying, Lord Jesus, receive my spirit. And he kneeled down, and cried with a loud voice, Lord, lay not this sin to their charge. And when he had said this, he* *fell asleep. <u>And Saul was consenting unto his death.</u> And at that time there was a great persecution against the church which was at Jerusalem; and they were all scattered abroad throughout the regions of Judaea and Samaria, except the apostles.)*

Let's look at the Apostles and how they sacrificed all for Christ, how they lived out the words of Paul in ***Philippians 1:21*** – *"For to me to live is Christ, and to die is gain"*. The following accounts of their deaths are either by historical records or by tradition handed down. One was slain in Ethiopia, one was dragged through the streets until he died, one was hanged, two were crucified, one upside down, one was flayed alive, one was pierced with lances until he died, one was thrown from the temple and beaten until he was dead, one was shot to death with arrows, one was stoned to death, and one was beheaded.[3]   As we study each Apostle we will get into who these individual deaths apply to.

This kind of hard persecution of the Church of Christ continued on for two more centuries and yet the Christian faith spread in that time to the whole known world. It went into all of the Roman Empire, Europe, Asia, Africa, England, and about everywhere else in the world at that time. The church was greatly persecuted, but the church was greatly flourishing in spite of the persecution.

JESUS AND THE TWELVE

(***Mark 3:14*** - *And he ordained twelve, that they should be with him, and that he might send them forth to preach,*) – Jesus called twelve men to be his disciples. He prayed before he called them. After he

---

[3] Carroll, J. (1931). *The Trail of Blood.* Challenge Press. - Page 11

called them, he ordained them for His work. They did not choose Jesus; He specifically chose them for the work He had for them to do. (*John 15:16 - Ye have not chosen me, but I have chosen you, and ordained you, that ye should go and bring forth fruit, and that your fruit should remain: that whatsoever ye shall ask of the Father in my name, he may give it you.*)

Jesus called his disciples into the ministry, but they generally were not what we would consider ministry ready. They were not polished, not great orators, did not possess a lot of natural ability to do what they were called to do. But they had one thing going for them; they were called into the ministry by Jesus Christ. If He if calls you, He will equip you with what you need to succeed. Not everyone is called to preach, but everyone is called to minister for Christ in some way. God delights in using those people for his ministry which would be the last ones chosen by men for the position. This ensures God gets the glory and not the man, because it is obvious that man could not, and is not dong it through his own abilities. (*I Corinthians 1:26 - For ye see your calling, brethren, how that not many wise men after the flesh, not many mighty, not many noble, are called*)

Everyone was not called to be an Apostle. It is generally accepted that an apostle was one who had to have been an eyewitness to the person of Christ.[4]

The twelve were instructed by Christ on how to fulfill their call. If you are a Christian, you have a call to ministry in your life. You need

---

[4] Malone, D. T. (1988). *The Apostles.* Murfreesboro, TN: Sword of the Lord Publishers.

to follow the example of the disciples in that they received instruction willingly. They knew they needed to be taught and willingly submitted to the teaching of God's word, so they would be equipped to better serve Him with their lives. (*Matthew 5:1-2 - And seeing the multitudes, he went up into a mountain: and when he was set, his disciples came unto him: And he opened his mouth, and taught them, saying,* & *Proverbs 19:20 - Hear counsel, and receive instruction, that thou mayest be wise in thy latter end.*)

The twelve were empowered to perform their ministry for Christ. (*Matthew 10:1 - And when he had called unto him his twelve disciples, he gave them power against unclean spirits, to cast them out, and to heal all manner of sickness and all manner of disease.*) The Apostles were given the power they needed to fulfill the ministry they were called, instructed and trained to do.

ORDINARY MEN

The Twelve were not well known. They were not the standouts; they were not the most popular people. They were your average everyday person like most of us are. History tells us that 11 out of the 12 of the disciples were from Galilee. The region of Galilee was generally considered less sophisticated, less educated, and less mannerly, and they apparently had an easily recognizable accent or manner of speech that would stand them out in a crowd as being from Galilee. The little girl at the trial of Jesus knew Peter was from Galilee by his speech. (*Mark 14:70 - And he denied it again. And a little after, they that stood by said again to Peter, Surely thou art one of them: for thou art a Galilaean, and thy speech agreeth thereto.*)

The Twelve were loved by Jesus. All of his disciples are loved by Him. All those that believe on his name are especially loved by Him. He prayed for his disciples. He also prayed for every one of us as He was praying for these twelve men. He prayed for you and me and it is recorded in the Gospel records that He did. (*John 17:20 - Neither pray I for these alone, but for them also which shall believe on me through their word;*)

The Apostles were ordinary men like you and me. They were called by Jesus into his service in the ministry. All but one lived their life for Him and His service. It is because of their zeal and willingness to give all for Christ and His work that you and I are here today to learn of Christ and have the opportunity to be saved. They helped found the Christian church. They proclaimed the word of God with boldness and without compromise, we should do no less (*Acts 4: 31 - And when they had prayed, the place was shaken where they were assembled together; and they were all filled with the Holy Ghost, and they spake the word of God with boldness.*)

THE APOSTLE PETER

Matthew 16:16 – *"And Simon Peter answered and said, Thou art the Christ, the Son of the living God."*

The Apostle Peter always had something to say, rarely was he without words. They were not always the right words, but he was always speaking up.

The Apostle Peter was always mentioned first in every list of the Apostles, including the last listing of them found in *Acts 1:13-14* – *"And when they were come in, they went up into an upper room,* where abode both Peter, and James, and John, and Andrew, Philip, and Thomas, Bartholomew, and Matthew, James the son of Alphaeus, and Simon Zelotes, and Judas the brother of James. These all continued with one accord in prayer and supplication, with the women, and Mary the mother of Jesus, and with his brethren." Peter was mentioned as many times as the Apostle Paul in the New Testament. Each of them is mentioned in about 150 passages or verses. Peter wrote two books of the New Testament, I & II Peter. Peter lived and died quite an incredible life. Some people find it easy to criticize Peter for all his faults, but let's face it; Peter was mightily used of God. He performed many miracles in the Lords name, and many thousands upon thousands of people were saved under his preaching.

"Peter was genuinely converted, unusually controversial, amazingly colorful, deeply consecrated and completely human." **Warren Wiersbe** [5]

BIOGRAPHICAL OVERVIEW OF THE APOSTLE PETER

Peter was from Bethsaida (*John 1:44*) which is on the banks of the Jordan River almost where it empties out into the Dead Sea. Peters birth name was Simon and his father's name was John or Jonah *"Simon bar Jonah"* (*Matthew 16:17*)

As a young man, he undoubtedly went to work as a fisherman on the Sea of Galilee. According to French historian, *Henri Daniel-Rops,* fishermen at this time on the Sea of Galilee, used two different kinds

---

[5] Cummings, D. G. (2008). *A Study of the Twelve Apostles.* Mustang, OK: Tate Publishing.

of nets. One circular, with weights attached, they would cast at a school of fish, and the other kind was called a *sagene,* this was on a band about 1500 feet long and 12 feet deep, this was a dragnet.[6] This is what was cast into the sea by the command of Jesus that was overflowing with fish and nearly sank their boat. (*John 21:6 – And he said unto them, Cast the net on the right side of the ship, and ye shall find. They cast therefore, and now they were not able to draw it for the multitude of fishes.*)

Peter was married; if he was the first Pope, which he most assuredly was not, he was not celibate. (*Matthew 8:14 -And when Jesus was come into Peter's house, he saw his wife's mother laid, and sick of a fever, & Mark 1:30, Luke 4:38 & I Corinthians 9:5*)

By about 28 A.D., Peter and his wife were living in Capernaum on the north shore of the Sea of Galilee, on the west side of the Jordan River. He owned his own boat by this time in partnership with Andrew, his brother, and James, and John the sons of Zebedee (*Matthew 4:18*)

Pentecost (*Acts 2:14-41*) – Peter preached the first Christian sermon on the day of Pentecost and 3,000 people were saved. (*Acts 2:14 - But Peter, standing up with the eleven, lifted up his voice, and said unto them, Ye men of Judaea, and all ye that dwell at Jerusalem, be this known unto you, and hearken to my words: & verse 41 - Then they that gladly received his word were baptized: and the same day there were added unto them about three thousand souls.*) Peter

---

[6] Ruffin, C. B. (1970). *The Twelve - The Lives of the Apostles After Calvary.* Huntington, IN: Our Sunday Visitor Publishing.

demonstrated tremendous boldness and power in his preaching this day. He was mightily used of God.

Peter preached openly in the temple (*Acts 3:11-12 - And as the lame man which was healed held Peter and John, all the people ran together unto them in the porch that is called Solomon's, greatly wondering. And when Peter saw it, he answered unto the people, Ye men of Israel, why marvel ye at this? or why look ye so earnestly on us, as though by our own power or holiness we had made this man to walk? & 4:4 - Howbeit many of them which heard the word believed; and the number of the men was about five thousand.)* – 5,000 people were saved this time. Remember, this again was taking place not that long after his greatest mistake (his denial of Christ at the fire), when he was at his lowest, he had no idea how high a mountain top Jesus had in mind for him not that far into the future.

Numerous other Miracles – All throughout the book of Acts we read of miracles performed by the Apostle Peter. (*Acts 5:12-15 - And by the hands of the apostles were many signs and wonders wrought among the people; (and they were all with one accord in Solomon's porch. And of the rest durst no man join himself to them: but the people magnified them. And believers were the more added to the Lord, multitudes both of men and women.)Insomuch that they brought forth the sick into the streets, and laid them on beds and couches, that at the least the shadow of Peter passing by might overshadow some of them.*)

- Aeneas had been bound to his bed for eight years "*sick of the palsy*". (*Acts 9:34 - And Peter said unto him, Aeneas, Jesus*

Christ maketh thee whole: arise, and make thy bed. And he arose immediately.)

- A woman named Tabitha, the Bible says she "*was full of good works*", had died. Peter was told about her death and he hurried to where her body had been laid. (***Acts 9:40-41*** *- But Peter put them all forth, and kneeled down, and prayed; and turning him to the body said, Tabitha, arise. And she opened her eyes: and when she saw Peter, she sat up. And he gave her his hand, and lifted her up, and when he had called the saints and widows, presented her alive.*)

Arrest by Herod (***Acts 12:1-11***) we find in this passage that Peter was arrested by Herod, who had just recently executed James, the brother of John. Herod took extreme measures to secure his prisoner Peter. In verse 4 it says, Peter was delivered to four quaternions of soldiers. A quaternion consisted of *"Four soldiers in each quaternion,... two on the inside with the prisoner (chained to him) and two on the outside, in shifts of six hours each, sixteen soldiers in all, the usual Roman custom."*[7]

Herod dispatched four quaternions or sixteen soldiers in all just to secure Peter. Peter was personally chained to two of them. Herod was keeping him in prison until after Easter, when he then intended to execute him. But, it was not Peter's time. An angel of the Lord appeared to Peter in the middle of the night and Peter's chains fell off and Peter was freed from prison and what Herod had planned for him.

---

[7] Marshall, I. H. (1983). *The Acts of the Apostles.* William B. Eerdmans.

DEATH OF PETER

John 21:18-19 – *"Verily, verily, I say unto thee, When thou wast young, thou girdedst thyself, and walkedst whither thou wouldest: but when thou shalt be old, thou shalt stretch forth thy hands, and another shall gird thee, and carry thee whither thou wouldest not. This spake he, signifying by what death he should glorify God. And when he had spoken this, he saith unto him, Follow me."*

"The Martyrdom of St. Peter" (1512)

Lucas Cranach (1472-1553)

Reliable historic tradition has it that Peter's manner of death was crucifixion.[8] The same manner of death as our Savoir. Jesus indicates this in the above passage when he says *"but when thou shalt be old, thou shalt stretch forth thy hands, and another shall gird thee, and carry thee whither thou wouldest not"*

Sixty to seventy years after the death of Peter, there are historical records indicating he was at Rome. Good people disagree on this point. Some say he was never in Rome, and others say he was in Rome. Most accounts of his death do not disagree on the manner of his death though.

The reliable traditional account of his death that indicates it took place in Rome, has it during the time of the persecution by Nero of Christians. Peter was in his 60's when he was crucified. Probably about A.D. 67. Peter was persuaded by believers in Rome to leave the city. They feared he would be martyred. On the edge of the city, tradition has it that Peter began to pray. Tradition has it as he prayed; Jesus appeared unto him and told him to come to Rome to be crucified again. Peter then realized what this meant that he, Peter, was to go back to Rome. There was to be another demonstration of one dying on the cross. Peter then turned around and went back to Rome. He was arrested then crucified. [9]

One more thing about Peter's crucifixion. Accurate tradition says Peter said as they were about to nail him to the cross *"I'm not worthy to die like Jesus died, on a cross with His head toward Heaven. In*

[8] Cummings, D. G. (2008). *A Study of the Twelve Apostles.* Mustang, OK: Tate Publishing.
[9] Malone, D. T. (1988). *The Apostles.* Murfreesboro, TN: Sword of the Lord Publishers.

all things that He might have the preeminence. I can't die like that, turn me upside-down" – Peter was then crucified upside down. [10]

THE APOSTLE ANDREW

The Apostle Andrew's name means *"manly"*; many preachers and commentators call Andrew a man's man. Andrew was the very first of the Apostles to follow Jesus. He is often referred to as Simon Peter's brother, but Andrew was his own man. He was the first of the twelve Apostles' to acknowledge Jesus was the Christ. Andrew's personality was basically the opposites of Peters. Andrew was calm and considerate and naturally helpful; his brother Peter was impulsive, bold and brash. Peter was a leader and took charge of men, Andrew was a man that supported leaders, looked out for leaders and followed leaders.

BIOGRAPHICAL OVERVIEW OF THE APOSTLE ANDREW

Andrew was first a disciple of John the Baptist. Andrew was saved under the ministry of John the Baptist. (***John 1:35 & 40***) Andrew one day heard John preach *"Behold the Lamb of God, which taketh away the sin of the world. This is he of whom I said, After me cometh a man which is preferred before me: for he was before me"* Andrew turned and saw Jesus, and Andrew never looked back. That one look at Jesus was enough to change Andrew's life forever. Andrew was

---

[10] Mallone, D. T. (1988). *The Apostles.* Murfreesboro, TN: Sword of the Lord Publishers.

Simon Peter's brother and partnered with Peter and James and John in a fishing business. Andrew lived in Bethsaida.

Eusebius, an early church historian, states part of Andrew's preaching ministry was spent in Asia Minor north of the Black Sea ministering to the Scythians. History tells us these people were not very civilized when Andrew went to minister among them. The Jewish historian Josephus considered them *little different from wild beasts*". It was reported this group of people practiced cannibalism at this time in history. The country of Russia traces part of its origins to this group of people Andrew ministered to. Because of this, Andrew is known as the patron saint of Russia.

Andrew was widely reported by many accounts and sources to have spent the last part of his life ministering in Greece in the city of Patrae. Andrew arrived here sometime in the A.D. 50's and spent the rest of this life ministering here. During this time, it is reported he made trips to Corinth, Philippi, Sparta, Megara and Istanbul.

ANDREW'S DEATH

A reliable traditional account of his death is as follows: Andrew led to Christ the wife of a local Governor in the area of Greece he was living in. Her husband demanded she renounce her Christian faith but she would not. So the Governor was so mad at Andrew for leading his wife to Christ he ordered Andrew arrested. He was arrested sometime in the fall of A.D. 69. As had happened with Peter two years earlier his prison guards had to be regularly changed out due to Andrew winning them to Christ almost as soon as they were assigned to guard him. Finally, on or about November 28 A.D. 69, the local Governor Aegeates, ordered Andrew to be crucified by tying his hands and feet to what is known as a transverse cross[11] (which resembles an X) and not nailing him to it. The Governor hoping by not nailing him he would prolong his agony on the cross and inflict more punishment on Andrew this way. Tradition has it that Andrew lasted two days on the cross and for those two days as people walked by and he hung there he never stopped preaching Jesus until his last breath. He died by crucifixion approximately two years after his brother Peter died by being crucified upside down.

---

[11] Cummings, D. G. (2008). *A Study of the Twelve Apostles.* Mustang, OK: Tate Publishing.

"The Martyrdom of St. Andrew" (1512)

Lucas Cranach (1472-1553)

THE APOSTLE JAMES

This James is the brother of John who was also an Apostle. There is another Apostle with the name of James; he is James the son of Alphaues. There is yet another James spoken of in the New Testament and that James is the earthly half-brother of Christ. James and his brother John are known as the *"sons of thunder"* (***Mark 3:17*** - *And James the son of Zebedee, and John the brother of James; and he surnamed them Boanerges, which is, The sons of thunder*) They were "nicknamed" this by Jesus; perhaps because of their personality. Commentators suggest James had a very passionate and enthusiastic personality and that once he believed in something he was very excited, zealous and forceful about those beliefs. We need more of this kind of Christian; ones who are excited, zealous and not timid about their Christian beliefs. James was also part of the inner circle of Christs. He was able to see, and experience somethings the other nine Apostles did not.

BIOGRAPHICAL OVERVIEW OF THE APOSTLE JAMES

He was the older brother of John. James along with John were part of a successful fishing business with Peter and his brother Andrew. James was also a native of Bethsaida in Galilee. James was present at Pentecost, but we don't hear or know much of his life or ministry after that until we have the account of his death.

THE DEATH OF JAMES

James was the first Apostle to be martyred, he was the third Christian martyr recorded in the Bible; the first being John the Baptist, the second Stephen and then James. His death was spoken of by Christ in **Mark 10:39** – *"And they said unto him, We can. And Jesus said unto them, Ye shall indeed drink of the cup that I drink of; and with the baptism that I am baptized withal shall ye be baptized:"* – James was the first Apostle to *"drink of the cup"* Jesus spoke of.

We find the account of his death recorded in **Acts 12:1-2** – *"Now about that time Herod the king stretched forth his hands to vex certain of the church. And he killed James the brother of John with the sword."* – Remember James asked for preeminence earlier, he got a very prominent place in the Apostles, he was the first of them to give his life for Christ. James was beheaded by order of Herod Agrippa. **James Elliot** a missionary that was killed by South American Indians in the 1950's said *"He is no fool who gives what he cannot keep, to gain what he cannot lose"* – The Apostle James did just that, he sacrificed his life for the cause of Christ.

THE APOSTLE JOHN

John 13:23 – *"Now there was leaning on Jesus' bosom one of his disciples, whom Jesus loved."*

The Apostle John enjoyed a special closeness to the Savior. It is said of him that he is the "Apostle of Love". He spoke of love more than 80 times in his writings. His name means "whom Jehovah loves". When John uses the word love it is more than a feeling though. It is a principle, it has power, it is a life changing person transforming virtue that comes from God Himself because as the Apostle John once told us in *I John 4:8* – *"He that loveth not knoweth not God; for God is love."*

John was probably the youngest of the Apostles, and he was also the last one to die. John was probably in his early twenties, possibly even in his late teens when he became a disciple of Christ. John had a very close intimate relationship with Jesus. He became close to the Lord by spending time with Him; like we can today through Bible reading and prayer. John was James' younger brother, one of the "Sons of Thunder". He went from being a "Son of Thunder" to the Apostle of Love. How could such a dramatic transformation take place? None other than by the transforming power Jesus has on a life that will surrender to Him and spend time learning His words and developing a relationship with Him, could produce this transformation. John was a member of the "inner circle" along with Peter and James, his brother, which were able to experience a more intimate relationship with Christ than the other nine Apostles did.

BIOGRAPHICAL OVERVIEW OF THE APOSTLE JOHN

John was a fisherman from Bethsaida. He was in a fishing partnership along with his brother James, Peter and Andrew before he was called by Jesus. (*Matthew 4:21-22*)

Jesus entrusted John with the care of his mother Mary at the cross. (*John 19:25-27*)

He wrote more of the New Testament than anyone else, except for the Apostle Paul. John was the human writer of five books of the New Testament.

- *The Gospel of John*

- *I, II, III John*

- *Revelation*

The Apostle John was later exiled to the Isle of Patmos for punishment for continuing to preach and teach the word of God. (*Revelation 1:9* - *I John, who also am your brother, and companion in tribulation, and in the kingdom and patience of Jesus Christ, was in the isle that is called Patmos, for the word of God, and for the testimony of Jesus Christ*)

John was the Apostle that had the privilege of serving Jesus the longest on earth.

JOHN'S DEATH

It is commonly reported that the Apostle John died a natural death; the only Apostle to do so. He died when he was about ninety-seven years old after much time spent exiled on the Isle of Patmos. It was while on this Island that John received the vision from the Lord Jesus that became the book of Revelation. (*Revelation 1:10-11a* - *I was in the Spirit on the Lord's day, and heard behind me a great voice, as of a trumpet, Saying, I am Alpha and Omega, the first and the last: and, What thou seest, write in a book, and send it unto the seven churches which are in Asia;*)

THE APOSTLE PHILLIP

John 1:43 *– "The day following Jesus would go forth into Galilee, and findeth Philip, and saith unto him, Follow me."*

The Apostle Phillip had the distinction of being the first Apostle that Jesus told to "*Follow me*". Phillip is only mentioned three times in Matthew, Mark and Luke; the three times he is mentioned is just in the list of the Apostles in each book. He is mentioned however enough in the book of John, so we can get a glimpse of his character. We get enough of a glimpse to pick up the slant of his personality and characteristics of his behavior, how he thought about things, so we can piece together a portrait of the man. Again, like the previous disciples we have studied, he was an ordinary man chosen and enabled by God to do extraordinary things for His service. Phillip was one of the Apostles, one of the men who helped change the world, the Bible tells us the Apostles turned the world upside down; but before we can change the world for God we need to let God change us first. (***Acts 17:6*** *- And when they found them not, they drew Jason and certain brethren unto the rulers of the city, crying, These that have turned the world upside down are come hither also;)*

BIOGRAPHICAL OVERVIEW OF THE APOSTLE PHILLIP

- Phillip was from Bethsaida (***John 1:44*** *- Now Philip was of Bethsaida, the city of Andrew and Peter.*)

- Phillip is one of three Phillip's mentioned in the New Testament. Phillip the tetrarch (*Luke 3:1*), Phillip the deacon (*Acts 6:5*) were the other two.

- Nothing is said about Phillip after *Acts 1:14*. We will not be able to look at anything he did after this time. Very little recorded information about Phillip exists after this that is reliable at all.

THE DEATH OF PHILLIP

We cannot with any real certainty talk about the death of the Apostle Phillip. Legendary accounts have him being crucified upside down like Peter. Most all accounts of his death though state he was martyred for his faith and witness for Christ. In *The Trail of Blood* by *JM Carroll* it reports that he was crucified and stoned.

Chapter Two Key Fundamental Principles:

1.) <u>Key Fundamental</u> – **Great Commission**. Through our accounts of the Apostles we see the fervency they all demonstrated in fulfilling the command of the Great Commission. They took this command very seriously. A good question to ask ourselves is do we take it just as seriously?

2.) <u>Key Fundamental</u> - **Faithfulness**. Another key fundamental we can glean from the lives of the Apostles, we have just studied, is the key fundamental of faithfulness. They did not let anything deter them from the call of their lives for Christ. Do we, perhaps from time to time, let circumstances of life temporarily derail us from the things of the Lord?

THE APOSTLES – Part 2

John 1:49 – *"Nathanael answered and saith unto him, Rabbi, thou art the Son of God; thou art the King of   Israel."*

THE APOSTLE NATHANAEL

Nathanael was also known as Bartholomew in the other three gospels. It is only in the book of John he is referred to as Nathanael. Many believe Bartholomew was his last name and Nathanael his first. Nathanael was a skeptic, but Jesus can save skeptics too. Nathanael was a religious man. There will be millions of people in heaven but there will also be millions of religious people who never made it to heaven. Being religious does not get you to heaven; accepting Jesus Christ by faith as your personal Savior does. Only ten verses in all four gospels contain his name. Nathanael was chosen by Christ. He was brought to Christ by Phillip. Have you brought anyone to Christ? (*II Corinthians 5:20* - *Now then <u>we are ambassadors for Christ</u>, as though God did beseech you by us: we pray you in Christ's stead, be ye reconciled to God.*)

BIOGRAPHICAL OVERVIEW OF THE APOSTLE NATHANAEL

Nathanael was from Cana. It is about eight miles northeast of Nazareth *John 21:2* – *"and Nathanael of Cana in Galilee."* This was where Jesus performed his first miracle. (*John 2:9-11*)

Nathanael means *"gift of God"*, Bartholomew means *"son of Tolmai"*

The Apostle Phillip was a friend of Nathanael's, and it was Phillip who brought him to Jesus. Are you bringing others to Jesus like Phillip did?

Four different historians all hold that Nathanael went on to minister in Armenia. The area of the Armenian Kingdom today is divided among the nations of Turkey, Iran, Iraq, and parts of the former Soviet Union. The historical accounts are that Nathanael was one of several disciples who ministered in this area at some point in time, but Nathanael seemed to stay here the longest of any of them.

The other area of ministry contributed to Nathanael is in the country of India. The account of his ministry here is brief and not as firm as his record of ministry in Armenia. Strong tradition is what we have for this phase of his ministry, not historical records; but this aspect of his life was thoroughly researched for validity by Indian Scholar A.C. Perumalil. He did extensive study of coins and other archeological artifacts of this timeframe, and based on this research, in his opinion, he pronounced this account of Nathanael's ministry essentially true. [12]

- This account of his ministry in India states he ministered in an area of India later called *"Happy India"* on the west coast of India. A.C. Perumalil found evidence of a flourishing Christian community here in the 6th century. [13]

- In A.D. 180, a copy of the Gospel of Matthew, written in Hebrew, was reported to have been found by a Christian visitor in *"Happy India"* to that person's amazement. Proof that at least someone of Hebrew decent had been there many years earlier witnessing for Christ.[14]

THE DEATH OF NATHANAEL

There are two slightly different traditional accounts of his death. They both state he was martyred while ministering in India. By both accounts he had only ministered there for no more than a couple years and was seeing many converts for Christ. The local governor was favorable to his ministry; it is said he had helped the governor's daughter greatly. The king of the area however did not appreciate Nathanael converting the locals to Christianity. Both accounts of his death state he was skinned alive. Both accounts differ on the final cause of his death. One says he was skinned alive, beaten brutally, then beheaded. The other account states he was skinned alive, beaten

---

[12] Ruffin, C. B. (1970). *The Twelve - The Lives of the Apostles After Calvary.* Huntington, IN: Our Sunday Visitor Publishing.
[13] (Ruffin, 1970)
[14] Both Eusebius and Jerome spoke of a Scholar named Pantanaeus who reported of this account as historically true.

brutally, then crucified. Both accounts put the date of his death in the early 60's A.D.

THE APOSTLE THOMAS

John 20:27-28 – "Then saith he to Thomas, Reach hither thy finger, and behold my hands; and reach hither thy hand, and thrust it into my side: and be not faithless, but believing. And Thomas answered and said unto him, My Lord and my God."

The Apostle Thomas has been, and will always be known, as the doubting disciple. People refer to him as doubting Thomas. This goes to prove to you that you are, and will be known by your actions. Guard your testimony, guard your reputation. Make sure it is a good one.

All we know of the characteristics of Thomas comes from the book of John. He is mentioned in the four lists of the Apostles and then in eight scripture references in the book of John. *Dr. Thomas Malone* said, *"God takes great truths from the Bible and clothes them around human personalities."* Like the first time grace is mentioned in the Bible, it is mentioned in reference to Noah; *"But Noah found grace in the eyes of the LORD." Genesis 6:8.* When you think of a great example of faith and trust you think of Abraham, the Bible says *"Abraham believed God, and it was counted unto him for righteousness" Romans 4:3,* when you think of stedfastness you think of Daniel, when you think of human failure in the life of a Christian you think of David, and when you think of a person doubting God, you always think of Thomas first. [15]

BIOGRAPHICAL OVERVIEW OF THE APOSTLE THOMAS

Thomas is also known as Didymus. Thomas is Hebrew for "twin", and Didymus is Greek for "double", or "twin". Many believe these were both nicknames given to the Apostle. Many believe because of these names; Thomas may have indeed had a twin brother.

Thomas' reputation to Christians some 2000 years after the fact, is as a doubter of the Lord, a doubter of the power of God. He did not believe Jesus was raised from the dead. This means he doubted the almighty power of God over problems, situations, life, and death.

It is reliably reported that most of the Apostle Thomas' ministry took place outside of the Roman Empire. It is reported, like Nathanael, he too ministered in the Armenian Kingdom and India. Though the reports about India are traditional not historical. Most of his ministry was said to have taken place in parts of modern-day Turkey, the Armenian Kingdom and Persia.

Thomas' besetting sin was the sin of doubt. We have all doubted at some point in time in our life. We have all questioned the ways of God at some point in time in our life. The key is to not stay there in that doubt, to not wallow in it, to recognize it for what it is and choose to exercise faith, choose to believe God, and choose to trust

---

[15] Malone, D. T. (1988). *The Apostles.* Murfreesboro, TN: Sword of the Lord Publishers.

God and His promises. Claim a promise of God from His Word and pray it back to Him.

THE DEATH OF THOMAS

Tradition tells us that Thomas died while he was preaching. It says he was preaching in India or Babylon and while he was preaching someone thrust him through with a lance and he died a martyr for Christ as he was preaching the Gospel of Christ.

"The Martyrdom of St. Thomas" (1512)

Lucas Cranach (1472-1553)

THE APOSTLE MATTHEW

Luke 5:27-28 – *"And after these things he went forth, and saw a publican, named Levi, sitting at the receipt of custom: and he said unto him, Follow me. And he left all, rose up, and followed him."*

The Apostle Matthew, also known as Levi, immediately answered the call of Christ on his life and left all to follow Him. We should also not hesitate to answer the call of God on our lives.

Matthew was probably the least most likely of all men to be called by Christ to be a disciple of His. Matthew was a publican; he was a tax collector. Most tax collectors at this time were not honest men. Roman tax collectors were usually wealthy men. They would buy a certain territory from Rome to get the right to collect taxes in it. The Roman government cared little about the tactics used to collect the taxes; they just cared that they were collected. The tax collectors were highly motivated to over collect taxes because they could keep the extra for themselves.

Dr. Tom Malone had this to say about Matthew - *"God likes to take a nobody and make a somebody out of him. He is just like a junk dealer; He goes around looking for something, finds it, shines it up and uses it. Then folks say it must be God"* [16]

BIOGRAPHICAL OVERVIEW OF THE APOSTLE MATTHEW

---

[16] Malone, D. T. (1988). *The Apostles.* Murfreesboro, TN: Sword of the Lord Publishers.

His surname was Levi. This may indicate he was of the tribe of Levi the priestly tribe. The priests of the tribe of Levi were to be collecting tithes of the Lord; they were not to be collecting taxes. (***Deuteronomy 10:8 & Hebrews 7:5***)

He was the son of Alphaeus – ***Mark 2:14*** – *"And as he passed by, he saw <u>Levi the son of Alphaeus</u> sitting at the receipt of custom, and said unto him, Follow me. And he arose and followed him."* This may indicate he was the brother of the Apostle James the Less (***Luke 6:15*** *- Matthew and Thomas, <u>James the son of Alphaeus</u>, and Simon called Zelotes,*) but this linkage is not conclusive.

Matthew dwelled in or near the city of Capernaum (***Mark 2:1, 13, 14***) it is not certain that he was born in this location.

Matthew was the human writer of the Gospel of Matthew. This Gospel presents Christ as King. The book of Matthew is generally considered the most popular and widely read of the four Gospels. Matthew's gospel is the book that links the Old Testament with the New Testament. Matthew cites Old Testament prophecies being fulfilled by Jesus multiple times throughout the book of Matthew.

It is reported that Matthew ministered to Jewish converts in Palestine eventually ending up in Ethiopia where he also ministered.

THE DEATH OF MATTHEW

Not much is known conclusively about the death of the Apostle Matthew. We have accounts of him finishing out his ministry in Ethiopia. Here is where the accounts of his martyrdom take place. There are too many varying accounts of how he was killed to place much confidence in any one in particular. One account has him being pierced with a sword until he died, another one has him being burned to death, and another has him being crucified. Though they do all agree he was martyred and that it probably took place in Ethiopia.

THE APOSTLE JAMES

The Apostle James, known as James the less, does not have much written about him in the New Testament. That does not mean he did not serve God greatly. He still was an Apostle, one of the twelve. The Holy Spirit for some reason just did not include much about his life in the scriptures.

James, the less, is the least known of all the Apostles. His name only occurs in the list of the Apostles. No particular word or deed is attributed to him. His nickname "the less" comes from the Greek work '*mikros*', which means small. It is believed James had a small stature and that he was the shortest of all the Apostles.

BIOGRAPHICAL OVERVIEW OF THE APOSTLE JAMES, THE LESS

His mother's name was Mary and his father's name was Cleophas (Hebrew) and Alpheus (Greek). Alpheus was the name of the father of the Apostle Matthew, which could mean James was Matthew's brother, though this link is not conclusive.

A man named Cleophas was one of the disciples whom Jesus met on the road to Emmaus after His resurrection. James' father could have been this Cleophas. (*Luke 24:13, 15, 18*)

His birth location is unknown. He is believed to have been from the area around Capernaum, but this too is also uncertain.

THE DEATH OF JAMES THE LESS

There are two different accounts of his death. Both accounts, he was killed in his service to Christ. Both have the location probably being Jerusalem. One account, he is thrown from the top of the temple and beaten to death[17], the other account has him being stoned to death by a mob of irate Jews.

---

[17] Carroll, J. (1931). *The Trail of Blood.* Challenge Press.

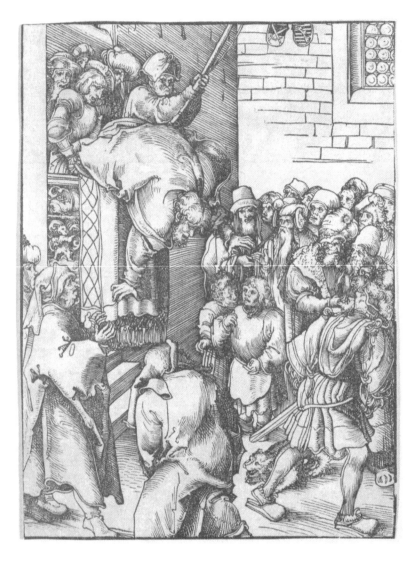

"The Martyrdom of St. James the Minor" (1512)

Lucas Cranach (1472-1553)

THE APOSTLE JUDAS, NOT ISCARIOT

The Apostle Judas, not Iscariot, does not have much recorded about him in the scriptures. Some Christians are called to not be in the lime light. Some are called to be in the background taking care of things no one may ever notice. These kinds of Christians are just as important as all the rest.

We only read of him speaking one time in the four Gospels. His only recorded words are found in *John 14:22* *"Lord, how is it that thou wilt manifest thyself unto us, and not unto the world?"* His one recorded question was a very thoughtful and doctrinally deep question though. It concerns the coming of the Holy Spirit also known as the Comforter. How could God *"manifest"* (from Greek *'emphanizo'* which means to exhibit in person or disclose by words, to appear, declare, inform, show and signify) if he was leaving them soon? The only way that is possible is to have the third person of the Trinity to come and live within or *"manifest"* himself within every saved person.

BIOGRAPHICAL OVERVIEW OF THE APOSTLE JUDAS, NOT ISCARIOT

He has two other names besides Judas. They are Lebbaeus and Thaddaues. Reliable legend has Judas preaching in Edessa (now called Urfa), Armenia, Ararat and modern-day Iran.

THE DEATH OF JUDAS, NOT ISCARIOT

The accounts of the Apostle Judas' death are pretty reliable. There are no varying accounts of different possible deaths or locations.

They all agree in the manner and most agree in the location of his death. It is said he angered local pagan priests and that he was shot to death with arrows as a result of this near Ararat which is in the eastern part of the country of Turkey.

THE APOSTLE SIMOM ZELOTES

Galatians 4:18 – *"But it is good to be zealously affected always in a good thing, and not only when I am present with you."*

Simon the Zelotes is primarily thought of in regard to being zealous about the things of God. There are eight other Simon's mentioned in the New Testament, one of them was Simon Peter, an Apostle. The Apostle Simon Zelotes also had the nickname of Simon the Canaanite. The Canaanite may have been an indication of where he was from, but most likely it was derived from the Hebrew word "kana" which means "Jealous".

OVERVIEW OF SIMON ZELOTES

Simon was apparently known for being very passionate, enthusiastic or zealous about what he did and about the things of God. (*Luke 6:15*) Having a zeal for the things of God like Simon did is a good thing. Paul was zealous about the things of the Lord as well in *I Corinthians 14:12* he said, *"Even so ye, forasmuch as ye are zealous of spiritual gifts, seek that ye may excel to the edifying of the church."*

MINISTRY AND DEATH OF SIMON ZELOTES

We do not have real reliable information about his ministry or his death. There is mention of him in some historical records that he ministered in Persia. There are also records that he was crucified. There is also an account that he died a natural death. These records are from limited sources and cannot be thought of as that reliable.

THE APOSTLE PAUL

I Corinthians 1:18 – *"For the preaching of the cross is to them that perish foolishness; but unto us which are saved it is the power of God."*

The Apostle Paul's life falls in line with this verse he wrote to the Corinthians. For the first part of his life the preaching of the cross was foolishness to him. He could personally testify of this fact. But when he was saved, the preaching of the cross took on the power of God to him and in his life.

When discussing the Apostle Paul, one cannot over emphasize the impact he had on the growth and development of the early church. He was a critically needed Apostle and an incredibly influential one. His conversion provided an incredible testimony of the saving, life transforming power of Jesus Christ. His missionary journeys led to the establishment of churches throughout the Mediterranean world. He is known as the *"Apostle to the Gentiles"*. He helped widen the door to the Gentiles after Peter first opened it. He left a big imprint on the Holy Scriptures. He wrote 13 (14 if you count *Hebrews*) books of the New Testament. In the history of the early church that Luke wrote, *"The Acts of the Apostles"*, Luke devoted the majority of it to the ministry of Paul. Paul was a mighty man of God, mightily used of God, to do mighty things for God.

BIOGRAPHICAL OVERVIEW OF SAUL

Saul was born in Tarsus in Cilicia around 5 AD. (*Acts 21:39, 22:3. 23:34*) Tarsus was a Roman province in SE Asian Minor (modern day Turkey). Tarsus was a capital city known for its school of literature and philosophy which was said to rival the schools in Athens and Alexandria. It is said Paul most likely attended this school while living in Tarsus. (*Acts 21:39 - But Paul said, I am a man which am a Jew of Tarsus...*)

Tarsus was a thriving business hub. It was a free city, and a city that enjoyed favor with Rome, so much so, that its residences were bestowed Roman citizenship. This explains why Paul could claim Roman citizenship and explains his comments in *Acts 22:27-28* – *"Then the chief captain came, and said unto him, Tell me, art thou a Roman? He said, Yea. And the chief captain answered, With a great sum obtained I this freedom. And Paul said, But I was free born."*

Saul was of pure Jewish ancestry. (*I Corinthians 11:22 - Are they Hebrews? so am I. Are they Israelites? so am I. Are they the seed of Abraham? so am I.*) He was of the tribe of Benjamin. (*Romans 11:1*) He was born a son of a Pharisee.

Saul's education. All the other Apostles were less educated than Paul. (*Acts 4:13 - Now when they saw the boldness of Peter and John, and perceived that they were unlearned and ignorant men...*)

– Saul/Paul was very well educated. His early educational opportunities were literally among the best, if not the best in the whole world at this time.

- Commentators say there are frequent indications and allusions in his writings to the classical literature of his time.

- Saul more than likely attended the school of literature and philosophy in Tarsus.

- Saul then traveled to Jerusalem and finished his education at the feet of Gamaliel. This would be a supreme education and honor for a Hebrew at this time to get educated by the great Rabbi Gamaliel. (*Acts 22:3 - I am verily a man which am a Jew, born in Tarsus, a city in Cilicia, yet brought up in this city at the feet of Gamaliel... & Acts 5:34 - Then stood there up one in the council, a Pharisee, named Gamaliel, a doctor of the law, had in reputation among all the people...*)

Saul's vocation. He was also trained in tent making. He used this skill to help sustain him in his mission work. (*Acts 18:3*)

Saul's religiousness. He was a strict Pharisee. (*Philippians 3:5 - Circumcised the eighth day, of the stock of Israel, of the tribe of Benjamin, an Hebrew of the Hebrews; as touching the law, a Pharisee*)

Saul was a persecutor of the Church (*Acts 26:9-11*)

Conversion of Saul – Saul's life and his name was forever changed as a result of an encounter with Jesus on the road to Damascus. (*Acts 9:1-6 – And Saul, yet breathing out threatenings and slaughter against the disciples of the Lord, went unto the high priest, And desired of him letters to Damascus to the synagogues, that if he found any of this way, whether they were men or women, he might bring them bound unto Jerusalem. And as he journeyed, he came near Damascus: and suddenly there shined round about him a light from heaven: And he fell to the earth, and heard a voice saying unto him, Saul, Saul, why persecutest thou me? And he said, Who art thou, Lord? And the Lord said, I am Jesus whom thou persecutest: it is hard for thee to kick against the pricks. And he trembling and astonished said, Lord, what wilt thou have me to do? And the Lord said unto him, Arise, and go into the city, and it shall be told thee what thou must do.*)

"Saul's Conversion"

Gustave Dore (1832-1833)

PAUL'S EARLY CHRISTIAN LIFE AND SERVICE

Paul's conversion likely took place around 36 A.D. His first missionary journey began nine years later. What was he doing in this nine-year time period? Knowing Paul's zeal for God, it was a time of preparation and active service locally for the Lord. If you want to serve the Lord full time with your life as a Pastor, Missionary or Evangelist you need to have a time of preparation and local service to get you ready for that calling. So too, Paul followed this path. He was called, today men are still called into God's service, Paul prepared, today men still need to prepare for God's service, Paul worked locally first, today men who are called by God need to be actively working in their local church first.

Immediately after his conversion Paul begins to preach. (*Acts 9:17-20*)

Paul did not stay in Damascus long after his conversion. (*Galatians 1:15-17*) Paul went to Arabia, a desert location southeast of Damascus. It is likely Paul stayed here the greater part of three years. (*Galatians 1:17b-18a - but I went into Arabia, and returned again unto Damascus. Then after three years*)

Paul's first visit to Jerusalem. At first the Church is afraid to receive him. (*Acts 9:26 - And when Saul was come to Jerusalem, he assayed to join himself to the disciples: but they were all afraid of him, and believed not that he was a disciple.*)

- Paul was eventually accepted by the church and he spent fifteen days with the Apostle Peter, one can only imagine what was discussed between the two. (*Galatians 1:18*)

- Paul was given free access to preach in Jerusalem, and boldly preach he did. (*Acts 9:29a - And he spake boldly in the name of the Lord Jesus*)

- An attempt was made on his life while in Jerusalem. The brethren warned him and sent him to Tarsus. (*Acts 9:29b - 30*)

Paul spends five years in Syria and Cilicia (39-43 A.D.) – He returned to Tarsus, the place of his birth, and began preaching in the surrounding regions. Barnabas arrives, and Paul departs the area and heads to Antioch. (*Acts 11:25-26a*) During this year in Antioch Paul and Barnabas preach to many people.

Paul's second visit to Jerusalem – Paul visited Jerusalem the second time to bring relief to them. Jerusalem had been experiencing a famine and was in need. (*Acts 11:29*)

PAUL'S FIRST MISSIONARY JOURNEY

Paul has been preparing and training for several years for what the Lord had planned for his life. Now he embarks on his first missionary journey with Barnabas. He would take the gospel to regions that had not even heard of it yet. (*Romans 15:20-21 - Yea, so have I strived to preach the gospel, not where Christ was named, lest I should build upon another man's foundation: But as it is written, To whom he was not spoken of, they shall see: and they that have not heard shall understand.*)

As the Elders and Prophets were fasting and ministering to the Lord, the Holy Spirit told them to separate Barnabas and Saul for the work

He was calling them to. The Elders and Prophets then prayed and laid hands on them and sent them away. (*Acts 13:1-3*)

They first went to the Island of Cyprus and preached the word of God. They had John Mark with them at this time; he would go on to later write the Gospel of Mark. Paul started off going to the Synagogues first then he would reach out to the Gentiles.

Paul and Barnabas then went to the regions of Pamphylia, Pisidia, and Lycaonia (46-47 A.D.) – While at Pisidia Paul accepts an invitation to speak at the local Synagogue. (*Acts 13:14-16*) – <u>His message can be divided into the following points:</u>

- Review of God's dealings with Israel (*Acts 13:17-22*)

- Proclaiming that Jesus is the promised Savior (*Acts 13:23-26*)

- Jesus death and resurrection (*Acts 13:27-37*)

- Salvation, Forgiveness, and Justification come through Jesus (*Acts 13:38-39 - Be it known unto you therefore, men and brethren, that through this man is preached unto you the forgiveness of sins: And by him all that believe are justified from all things, from which ye could not be justified by the law of Moses.*)

- Ends with a warning not to fulfill prophecy by rejecting Christ (*Acts 13:40-41*)

Paul and Barnabas then go to Iconium, where an attempt to stone them forces them to leave. They then go onto Lystra and Derbe where Paul heals a lame man and the local residents attempt to worship Paul and Barnabas. (*Acts 14:8-18*)

They return home from this first missionary trip and report back to the church at Antioch on how God had opened a door to the Gentiles and blessed their efforts. They set a precedent by doing this that is still carried out today by missionaries. Missionaries go out for a few years and come back to report of their work to the local churches that sent them out on how the Lord has blessed them and used their efforts. (*Acts 14:27*)

PAUL'S SECOND MISSIONARY JOURNEY

After some time in Antioch, Paul begins to wonder about the brethren he had won to Christ and ministered to on his first missionary journey. So Paul sets out to go on his second missionary journey. Just like his first missionary journey, his second one begins at the church in Antioch. Paul and Barnabas disagree on whether to take John Mark with this time. John Mark had left them part way through their last journey and Paul thought him unreliable. So Paul selects Silas to travel with him this time and Barnabas takes John Mark with him to Cyprus. (*Acts 15:39-40*)

Paul and Silas head to Derbe and Lystra again. Here Paul desired Timothy to go with them. Timothy's mother was a Jew and his father was a Greek. (*Acts 16:1-3a*)

Paul and Silas were not permitted by the Holy Spirit to head toward Bithynia. (*Acts 16:7 - After they were come to Mysia, they assayed to go into Bithynia: but the Spirit suffered them not.*) – This should teach us to always be listening and willing to submit to the direction or nudging of the Holy Spirit in our life. Paul and Silas thought it best to go in one direction, but the Holy Spirit was leading them in a different direction. They did not quench the Holy Spirits leading in their life. They were attentive to it; they were open to it and wanted to follow Him. (*I Thessalonians 5:19* - *Quench not the Spirit.*)

We cannot cover all the events and circumstances that occurred on this second journey, but we will look at what happened at the City of Philippi.

- Lydia, the seller of purple, and her household were all saved. (*Acts 16:13-15*)

- Paul casts a demon out of a girl in the city of Philippi. (*Acts 16: 16*)

- Paul and Silas are beaten and imprisoned. (*Acts 16:19-24*)

- A miraculous earthquake occurs, and the Philippian jailor and his family get saved. (*Acts 16:25-34*)

- Luke, who had accompanied Paul and Silas, and also wrote the Gospel of Luke and the book of Acts, stays in Philippi along with Lydia and the Jailor and their families to start the work of building the church of Philippi.

Paul also visited Thessalonica, Berea (where it is noted they searched the Scriptures daily), Athens (where Paul's sermon on the "Unknown God" took place), and Corinth. Many were saved and baptized in Corinth. Many of the church of Corinth were saved out of deep sin. The ministry in Corinth teaches us that we should never write off anyone and consider them un-savable. God can do anything at any time. Keep praying for those who you think may be a lost cause. God can still save them out of their deep sin and He can do it up to their last breath. (*I Corinthians 6:11 - And such were some of you: but ye are washed, but ye are sanctified, but ye are justified in the name of the Lord Jesus, and by the Spirit of our God.*)

PAUL'S THIRD MISSIONARY JOURNEY

Paul's third missionary journey, he first went to Galatia and Phrygia where he ministered *"strengthening all the disciples"* in those local churches.

Ephesus – Paul stayed the better part of three years in Ephesus on his third missionary journey. Paul's efforts were greatly blessed during this time in Ephesus. (*Acts 19 & 20*)

- While in Ephesus, Paul taught in the Synagogue for three months and in the school of Tyrannus for three years (*Acts 19:8-10*)

- The Lord used him to work unusual miracles during this time. (*Acts 19:11-12 - And God wrought special miracles by the hands of Paul: So that from his body were brought unto the sick handkerchiefs or aprons, and the diseases departed from them, and the evil spirits went out of them.*)

- Paul wrote Galatians and I Corinthians while in Ephesus.

- Paul describes the kind of preaching he did while in Ephesus in *Acts 20:20-21, 26-27, 31)*. Paul preached the whole counsel of God to them. He kept nothing back. He went everywhere and from house to house declaring the message of repentance to God and faith toward Christ.

Macedonia – Paul went on to preach throughout Macedonia. The Macedonians are known for their generous giving to help others even when they needed things themselves. (*II Corinthians 8:1-2*) – We need to model their selfless giving of themselves, the Macedonian Christians had, in our life too.

Corinth – Paul then goes on to visit Corinth. Corinth was a work that required much instruction, direction, attention and admonishing from the Apostle. Paul was hoping and praying for a good visit with them but not necessarily expecting the visit to go well. (*I Corinthians 2:1-4*) Paul was always looking to be *"strengthening all the disciples"* with instruction, seasoned with love. He would admonish sternly if that is what was required of the situation; but it grieved Him to do so because of the great love he had for the lost and those new in Christ.

PAUL'S ARREST

Agabus prophesied of Paul's impending imprisonment in *Acts 21:10-11* – *"And as we tarried there many days, there came down from Judaea a certain prophet, named Agabus. And when he was come unto us, he took Paul's girdle, and bound his own hands and feet, and said, Thus saith the Holy Ghost, So shall the Jews at Jerusalem bind the man that owneth this girdle, and shall deliver him into the hands of the Gentiles."*

Paul's arrival into Jerusalem would of have been one of joyful anticipation because he wanted to be there for Pentecost. But it also would have been one of anxiousness because he knew what awaited him there. (*Acts 20:22-23 - And now, behold, I go bound in the spirit unto Jerusalem, not knowing the things that shall befall me there: <u>Save that the Holy Ghost witnesseth in every city, saying that bonds and afflictions abide me.</u>*)

Paul was arrested in the Temple. (*Acts 21:27-31)*

PAUL'S TRIALS AND IMPRISONMENTS

Paul defended himself in various trials; before the mob in Jerusalem (*Acts 21:37-22:29*) before the Sanhedrin (*Acts 22:30-23:10*) before Felix the governor in Caesarea (*Acts 23:11-24:27*) before Festus the governor in Caesarea (*Acts 25:1-12*) before King Herod Agrippa II in Caesarea (*Acts 25:13-26:32*) and eventually appealing all the way to Rome.

This phase of Paul's life would prove to be a time of prophetic fulfillment. For Paul would have the opportunity to preach Jesus to two Roman Governors, a Jewish King, and the household of Caesar, the most powerful man on the planet at this time. (*Acts 9:15 - But the Lord said unto him, Go thy way: for he is a chosen vessel unto me, to bear my name before the Gentiles, and kings, and the children of Israel*) – God can use a person surrendered to do His will in mighty, miraculous, and unexpected ways. We just need to be the willing vessel and let God work His will out in our life.

PAUL'S DEATH AND LASTING TESTIMONY

As the time of his death neared, Paul was expecting it. He was ready to be offered a sacrifice (*II Timothy 4:3*) Paul was not ashamed (*II*

Timothy 1:12) Paul was confident *(Philippians 1:21*) Paul was sure of his reward (*II Timothy 4:8*)

Although imprisoned, forsaken by some, and knowing his death was near, Paul was still triumphant. Paul said from that dungeon cell, "*Notwithstanding the Lord stood with me, and strengthened me; that by me the preaching might be fully known, and that all the Gentiles might hear: and I was delivered out of the mouth of the lion. And the Lord shall deliver me from every evil work, and will preserve me unto his heavenly kingdom: to whom be glory for ever and ever. Amen."* **II Timothy 4:17-18**. Paul also said these powerful words in the midst of dire and dreadful circumstances; his faith never wavered, his love never ran out, his confidence never faltered, *"For I am now ready to be offered, and the time of my departure is at hand. I have fought a good fight, I have finished my course, I have kept the faith:"* **II Timothy 4:6-7**.

Paul was beheaded in 67 or 68 A.D. Roman citizenship exempted him from torture and crucifixion. He was executed on a road just outside of Rome by a military escort.

Let's close out this section on Paul by reading his own words in *II Corinthians 11:23-33* – "*Are they Hebrews? so am I. Are they Israelites? so am I. Are they the seed of Abraham? so am I. Are they ministers of Christ? (I speak as a fool) I am more; in labours more abundant, in stripes above measure, in prisons more frequent, in deaths oft. Of the Jews five times received I forty stripes save one. Thrice was I beaten with rods, once was I stoned, thrice I suffered shipwreck, a night and a day I have been in the deep; In journeyings often, in perils of waters, in perils of robbers, in perils by mine own countrymen, in perils by the heathen, in perils in the city, in perils in the wilderness, in perils in the sea, in perils among false brethren; In weariness and painfulness, in watchings often, in hunger and thirst, in fastings often, in cold and nakedness. Beside those things that are without, that which cometh upon me daily, the care of all the churches. Who is weak, and I am not weak? who is offended, and I burn not? If I must needs glory, I will glory of the things which concern mine infirmities. The God and Father of our Lord Jesus Christ, which is blessed for evermore, knoweth that I lie not. In Damascus the governor under Aretas the king kept the city of the Damascenes with a garrison, desirous to apprehend me: And through a window in a basket was I let down by the wall, and escaped his hands."*

What a foundation that the Apostles help lay for the establishing of the church! We know Christ is the foundation of the church, but the work, the sacrifice, the testimony in life and in death from Christ's Apostles is astounding and awe inspiring to consider and meditate on. They literally gave all for Christ, they gave all for their fellow believers, they gave all for us too! Let's hope into the Fundamental DNA of every church is woven much of the faithful and zealous DNA of the Apostles.

"Paul's Shipwreck"

Gustave Dore (1832-1833)

Chapter Three Key Fundamental Principles:

1.) <u>Key Fundamental</u> – **Zeal for ministry**. The Apostles all set us an example of having a sincere zeal for the ministry. Do we have this same kind of zeal for ministry as the Apostles did?

2.) <u>Key Fundamental</u> – **Sacrificial ministry**. The Apostles all sacrificed willingly, and greatly for the cause of Christ. When we have to make any kind of sacrifice for the Lords work, like a little bit of time to help with a project, or a Saturday morning to help with visitation, or perhaps when we give monetarily, do we do it willingly, and think of it as a privilege to do so as the Apostles did?

3.) <u>Key Fundamental</u> – **The Power of Forgiveness**. Saul's conversion demonstrates to us the power of forgiveness in two ways: first he was forgiven by Christ, and secondly he was forgiven by the Christians he had been persecuting. When someone wrongs you, do you forgive them and not let bitterness well up in your heart, or do you perhaps hold onto that hurt and hold a grudge against that person?

4.) <u>Key Fundamental</u> – **Missions Minded.** All of the Apostles set the example of mission's mindedness. Paul set the pattern of how this was to work through the local church. Are you missions minded like the Apostles were? Do you support missions through your local church, do you pray for them? Do you go out into your own local mission field seeking the lost, with a fervent desire to see their salvation?

We all need to be. If you are not as missions minded as you should be, perhaps make that commitment to God right now in your heart that you will be from this point forward.

EARLY CHURCH ORIGINS

Fundamentalists do not believe in Apostolic succession. The office of the Apostle ceased to exist with the death of the Apostles. It was to the church that Christ promised continual existence, not to Peter or to the other Apostles, but it was to the church, which Christ was establishing, that He promised eternal existence to. Christ founded the church, He died for the church, He is the foundation of the church, and during His earthly ministry Christ said *"... I will build my church; and the gates of hell shall not prevail against it." Matthew 16:18*. Christ then went on and gave them the Great Commission, which tells them what His church is to do *"Go ye therefore, and teach all nations, baptizing them in the name of the Father, and of the Son, and of the Holy Ghost: Teaching them to observe all things whatsoever I have commanded you: and, lo, I am with you alway, even unto the end of the world. Amen." Matthew 28:19-20*.

OUR ORDERS AND HIS PROMISE

The origin of the church and its mission does not start with man but with Son of Man, Christ Jesus. His Great Commission was not given to the Apostles as individuals but to them and the coming church as a whole. The Apostles and others who heard Him give this Great Commission were all soon dead, but the Church, the Church has never died, it is as much alive now as it was at its inception by Christ. Yes, the church has been persecuted, the history of the church is awash in the blood of the saints, it survived the Dark Ages, it survived the persecution from the Catholic church, it survived, it survived, it survived, and it thrived. In the history of the church there seems to be a correlation of the church physically growing and spiritually thriving while under trial and persecution.

The church yes has also gone through much heresy, it has had many false teachers who have *"crept in unawares"*, trying to deceive and sadly doing just that to many people, but the church is still here, the true church is still here. There has always been a remnant left of true believers to carry on the message, the greatest message in the history of the world, and that is salvation by grace through faith in the One who so loved the world so completely and perfectly, that He came down and died for all sin, for all mankind that we may, just by accepting this payment in full on the cross on our behalf, receive the gift of eternal life through Jesus Christ our Lord and Savior.

This history, this great testimony of the church, shows to us that the Lords promise has been fulfilled when He said, *"the gates of hell shall not prevail against it."* Well Hell and Satan have sure tried to prevail against it, but they NEVER have, and they NEVER will prevail against it, if no other reason but that Jesus said they would not. This simple fact should reassure us into the surety of all the promises of the Lord. If God said it, then we can believe it, trust in it, and live our life by it. I would encourage you to claim all the promises of God in your life; for the Lord is true, He is faithful, He is righteous, and He is Love, pure perfect Love. (*II Peter 3:9 - The Lord is not slack concerning his promise, as some men count slackness; but is long-suffering to us-ward, not willing that any should perish, but that all should come to repentance.*) The Lord wants all men to be saved, He does not want any to perish. We have a great Lord, who loves the whole world, including you. We have a Lord who died for all, including you. We have a Lord who keeps all His promises, will never fail us, will never forsake us. Thinking of all of this, what are we doing for Him in comparison?

SOME BACKGROUND

What we know as Christianity today began with Jesus starting to establish His church before His ascension into Heaven and fully establishing it at Pentecost. It was founded within the bounds of the Roman Empire; the greatest empire the world has ever known. It stretched to most of the known world at that time. The Roman Empire built great roads and aqueducts. These great roads, along with the safety the Roman Army provided, made it much easier to travel and for news to spread abroad. It was perfectly fertile ground and circumstances for a new faith to come on the scene and be established and then spread around the world. It was not coincidence the church age was introduced into this setting; it was planned this way before the foundation of the world. (*Ephesians 1:3-7 - Blessed be the God and Father of our Lord Jesus Christ, who hath blessed us with all spiritual blessings in heavenly places in Christ: According as he hath chosen us in him before the foundation of the world, that we should be holy and without blame before him in love: Having predestinated us unto the adoption of children by Jesus Christ to himself, according to the good pleasure of his will, To the praise of the glory of his grace, wherein he hath made us accepted in the beloved. In whom we have redemption through his blood, the forgiveness of sins, according to the riches of his grace;)*

The main religions of the Roman Empire at this time were pagan; it was a religion of many gods. There were many devout believers and worshippers of these gods. This was a religion not just of the people, but it was the religion of the empire, protected by law and supported by the government. It was the established religion.

The Jewish people were no longer a separate people, they had been conquered and were part of this Roman Empire. Yet they still had their temple in Jerusalem and still went there to worship. They were also very jealous of their religion. The pagan's religions and gods were not real and had no real power or ability to help them. The Jews on the other hand were worshipping the true God, but had turned their back on Him, rejecting His Son and their Messiah in favor of keeping the letter of their religious laws while going against the spirit of them. They were so puffed up with knowledge and what they were doing to project how religious they were, they did not recognize the Truth when He came and they rejected Him and had the Truth crucified.

Word of Warning: The Jews of this time and some Christians of our time have the same weakness in common. Some, not all by any means, but some who are, or who claim to be Christian, get too caught up in the projection of how Christian they are, or how good they are at acting the part, projecting the part, and looking the part of being a "Fundamentalist", that they do great disservice to the Truth and to themselves. It is much more important who we are on the inside then who we project to be on the outside. We all need to be on the lookout for this weakness in our character and seek to guard against this weakness. (*Mark 7:1-13 - Then came together unto him the Pharisees, and certain of the scribes, which came from Jerusalem. And when they saw some of his disciples eat bread with defiled, that is to say, with unwashen, hands, they found fault. For the Pharisees, and all the Jews, except they wash their hands oft, eat not, holding the tradition of the elders. And when they come from the market, except they wash, they eat not. And many other things there be, which they have received to hold, as the washing of cups, and pots, brasen vessels, and of tables. Then the Pharisees and scribes asked him, Why walk not thy disciples according to the tradition of the elders, but eat bread with unwashen hands? He answered and said unto them, Well hath Esaias prophesied of you hypocrites, as it is written, This people honoureth me with their lips, but their heart is far from me. Howbeit in vain do they worship me, teaching for doctrines the commandments of men. For laying aside the commandment of God, ye hold the tradition of men, as the washing of pots and cups: and many other such like things ye do. And he said unto them, Full well ye reject the commandment of God, that ye may keep your own tradition. For Moses said, Honour thy father and thy mother; and, Whoso curseth father or mother, let him die the death: But ye say, If a man shall say to his father or mother, It is Corban, that is to say, a gift, by whatsoever thou mightest be profited by me; he shall be free. And ye suffer him no more to do ought for his father or his mother; Making the word of God of none effect through your tradition, which ye have delivered: and many such like things do ye.*)

A BLOOD-SOAKED BEGINNING

Beginning with the cross and the crucifixion of Christ, the beginnings of the church saw a lot of bloodshed. Following the Savior over the next several years, the church saw many martyred heroes of the faith. The church was under hard persecution by Judaism and Paganism. Jesus had spoken to His followers of persecution to come. He made it no secret that following Him and doing His work would not be the easy road, but that it would require, dedication, hard work, and sacrifice. (***John 15:19-20*** - *If ye were of the world, the world would love his own: but because ye are not of the world, but I have chosen you out of the world, therefore the world hateth you. Remember the word that I said unto you, The servant is not greater than his lord. If they have persecuted me, they will also persecute you; if they have kept my saying, they will keep yours also.*)

EARLY ERRORS AND HERESY

Error already begins to creep into the church in this early time period in its history; and this is where Our Fundamental DNA starts to come into view at this point in church history. There have always been men, who have boldly stood for the fundamentals of the Christian faith, come what may. It is at this point we start to see the need to identify that fundamental character and fervor in some of our most ancient of church fathers. They saw the need to take the stand against the error, against the heresy, against the evil government and rulers of their day. If they had not stood true to the faith, think of the countless millions that most likely would not have been saved over the centuries since then. It is always important to stand for what is right, no matter the point in history and no matter the sacrifices that come along with that stand. (*Acts 5:29 - Then Peter and the other apostles answered and said, We ought to obey God rather than men.*)

After the last Apostle John died, the Church was left with the final inspired written record of the revealed will of God. There was no other infallible recourse for the Church and many views and different doctrines were being introduced. The lack of careful exegesis and agreed upon method of biblical interpretation resulted in a freedom to interpret the revelation of God in a way that best made sense to the interpreter, instead of being concerned about coming to the conviction of what the original author and Holy Spirit meant at the time of writing the inspired text.[18] It became more important what it meant to the interpreter, or even worse, the text was twisted to prove doctrines not taught in the text at all (i.e. the divine powers of the saints and Mary, infant baptism and others). By the early 2nd century, heretical doctrines such as baptismal regeneration were already being taught as essential to the faith. Other major doctrinal heresy's that were developing concerned the deity of Christ and the doctrine of salvation. These heresies had already begun to split the church wide open, but good men, men who believed in the fundamentals of our faith and doctrine were staying strong, taking stands and doing what they could to correct the errors and to keep fulfilling the orders from Christ to evangelize the whole world. (*II Timothy 4:4-5 - And they shall turn away their ears from the truth, and shall be turned unto fables. But watch thou in all things, endure afflictions, do the work of an evangelist, make full proof of thy ministry.*)

---

[18] Fanning, D. (2018, April 9th). *MIssions of the Early Church.* Retrieved from digitalcommons.liberty.edu:http://digitalcommons.liberty.edu/cgi/viewcontent.cgi?article =1001&context=cgm_hist

By the turn of the first century, less than 70 years after the crucifixion of Christ, Christianity was already strongly represented in Asia Minor, Syria, Macedonia, Greece, Rome and Egypt. By 113 A.D. a Roman Governor was complaining to the Emperor Trajan that Christianity was negatively affecting the temple worship. Much of what we know of the early church comes from the writings of the early church "fathers". These were church leaders whom were assumed to have been strongly influenced by the Apostles. Some of these early church leaders in addition to Polycarp were Clement, Barnabas, and Hermas. All of them wrote between 100 to 150 A.D. Also, during this time period there was an important document titled "The Teaching of the Twelve Apostles". *"These writings make it clear that many different ideas developed among Christians from the very beginning. They also make it clear that early Christians were united around the ideas of the basic fundamentals of the Christian faith. People who rejected those basics were not considered true Christians"* – **Dr. Phil Stringer**. [19]

J.M. Carroll in his book The Trail of Blood, stated this on early church heresy and how it crept into the church *"Let it be remembered that changes like these here mentioned were not made in a day, nor even within a year. They came about slowly and never within all the churches. Some of the churches vigorously repudiated them. So much so that in A.D. 251, the loyal churches declared non-fellowship for those churches which accepted and practiced these errors. And thus came about the first real official separation among the churches."*[20]

---

[19] Stringer, P. (2011). *The Faithful Baptist Witness.* Cleveland, GA: Old Paths Publications.
[20] Carroll, J. (1931). *The Trail of Blood.* Challenge Press.

SOME FUNDAMENTAL TRUTHS

Also, in the second century church there was much controversy over the sole authority of Scripture. Keep in mind, what we now know as the New Testament, the writings that comprise it had just recently been written. The Apostle John had still been receiving revelation from God not too far in the past from this moment in history. The books of the New Testament had all been written at this point, but not all the church fathers had all the portions of them. It is understandable, at this point in church history, there would not be total unity in faith and practice by all of those who were sincere to their fullest knowledge standing strong to the truths of Scripture.

In the early church there was a conflict over infant baptism. And this conflict demonstrates to us that this was a totally new idea that had crept into part of the church. It was very difficult for these new advocators of infant baptism to persuade many of these early churches to move away from baptism by immersion for believers only. *"All the (church) fathers of the first four ages, down to Jerome (A.D. 370), were of Greece, Syria and Africa, and though they give great numbers of histories of the baptism of adults, yet there is not one of the baptism of a child till the year 370."* (Compendium of Baptist History, Shackelford, p. 43; Vedder, p. 50; Christian, p, 31; Orchard, p. 50)[21] It should have been clear to all that infant baptism was not biblical and should not be practiced; but too many relied on the teachings of men and their thoughts on the subject. However, if they

---

[21] Carroll, J. (1931). *The Trail of Blood.* Challenge Press.

had been practicing the fundamental of the sole authority of Scripture this would not have occurred.

It is very clear that from the beginning of the church that there was much disagreement over its various doctrines. But what is also clear, with a fair assessment of the early church, is there can be seen fundamental ideas and beliefs pervading the early church as well. Being a fundamentalist in belief and practice is not a new thing at all. What is relatively new in church history is the word Fundamental being attached to those core beliefs and convictions.

God's Word is as relevant and needed in today's world more than ever. His Word is an enduring word (*I Peter 1:25a – But the word of the Lord endureth for ever.*). His Word is a living word. His Word is a guiding and molding word. His Word is an all-powerful word (*Hebrew 4:12 – For the word of God is quick, and powerful, and sharper than any two edged sword, piercing even to the dividing asunder of soul and spirit, and of the joints and marrow, and is a discerner of the thoughts and intents of the heart.*). The world needs God's Word. The Christian needs God's Word. The world we live in is increasingly rejecting and even mocking God and His Word. We live in a world that thinks God is old fashioned and out of style. But God's Word has the answers to all of life's problems and difficulties. Everything we need to get through life is found in the Word of God. His Word is life. *"Jesus saith unto him, I am the way, the truth, and the life: no man cometh unto the Father, but by me." John 14:6.*

"FUNDAMENTAL" CHURCH FATHERS

It would not be truthful to say that all the early church fathers were Fundamentalists like we think of the word today. But what is totally truthful is that all of the Fundamentals of the faith are as ancient as the church, there have been men all throughout the centuries of church history that could have been called Fundamentalists. For example, Polycarp does not write about all the specific fundamentals that we know today but concerning the ones he did write about he would be considered to be fundamental in his beliefs and teachings.

The earliest Church Fathers, (within two generations of the Twelve Apostles of Christ) are usually called the Apostolic Fathers since tradition describes them as having been taught by the twelve. Important Apostolic Fathers include Clement of Rome, Ignatius of Antioch, Polycarp of Smyrna, and Papias of Hierapolis. In addition, the Didache and Shepherd of Hermas are usually placed among the writings of the Apostolic Fathers although their authors are unknown; like the works of Clement, Ignatius and Polycarp, they were first written in Koine Greek.

Defining the Term - Koine Greek:

The fairly uniform Hellenistic Greek spoken and written from the 4th century BC until the time of the Byzantine emperor Justinian (mid-6th century AD) in Greece, Macedonia, and the parts of Africa and the Middle East that had come under the influence or control of Greeks or of Hellenized rulers. Based chiefly on the Attic dialect, the Koine had superseded the other ancient Greek dialects by the 2nd century AD. Koine is the language of the Greek translation of the Old Testament (the Septuagint), of

---

the New Testament, and of the writings of the historian Polybius and the philosopher Epictetus. It forms the basis of Modern Greek. [22]

ORIGIN OF THE NEW TESTAMENT CANON

The most fundamental necessity to our faith is an accurate collection of the inspired words of God. This was achieved over several centuries of time. We will briefly look at how we got our current New Testament. Starting with the original writings of the Apostles and those closely associated with them to our present-day King James version of the Bible, which is the Bible for English speaking people.

The New Testament consist of twenty-seven books that were written about AD 45-100. The books of the New Testament were originally written on leather scrolls, and papyrus sheets. [23] They were at first circulated as individual letters and not a collection as we know them now. One of the most widely circulated books of the New Testament was the Gospel of Matthew. The Apostle Paul specifically instructed that some of his letters were to be circulated (*Colossians 4:16 - And when this epistle is read among you, cause that it be read also in the church of the Laodiceans; and that ye likewise read the epistle from Laodicea.*) Various copies were eventually gathered together into collections. They were further copied into codices, which are similar to modern-day books, with the pages sewn together to form a binding.

<u>Setting the Stage for the New Testament</u>

---

[22] *Koine Greek Language*. (2018, September 17). Retrieved from Encyclopedia Britannica: https://www.britannica.com/topic/Koine-Greek-language

[23] Papyrus is thick paper material that comes from the center tissue of the papyrus plant.

Many different factors need to be addressed when considering the formation of the New Testament Canon. Canon refers to a permanent list of authoritative books that are recognized as Scripture[24]. "God-breathed" the writings of Scripture, through the Holy Spirit, so that the writers of Scripture wrote only the words of God without any error. The New Testament was written in Koine Greek, which differs from classical Greek. Archaeological discoveries have uncovered thousands of parchments of "common language Greek", verifying that God chose to use the language of the common people (Koine Greek) in the writing of the New Testament in order to communicate His revelation to the masses and not just a select highly educated few. Koine Greek is a very expressive language that is able to communicate minute details and nuances that no other language is able to do with as much precision. It was the perfect language to communicate His perfect word without error. Koine Greek was a widely used trade language of the world at the time of the writing of the New Testament. More people knew this language or had a familiarity with it than any other language. The New Testament, being written in this language made it immediately accessible to vast numbers of people.

The Manuscripts

We do not have the original manuscripts, or the ones signed by the Apostles themselves. The persecution of the Roman empire assured us of that. They thought if they could destroy the church's literature they could eliminate Christianity. God in His wisdom though, I believe, allowed the original manuscripts, the ones penned by the

---

[24] Barr, J. (1983). *Holy Scripture, Canon, Authority, Criticism.* Philadelphia, PA: Westminster.

Apostles and few others, to be destroyed so they would not turn into objects that are worshipped and venerated like "relics" from the Holy land, and supposedly from Christ or others are today. Not having the original manuscripts is not something we should be worried about, scholars who work with non-biblical documents of antiquity usually likewise do not have access to the originals.

When considering manuscript evidence, there is a significantly larger amount of evidence for biblical manuscripts than there are for other secular works. By comparing the manuscript support for the Bible with manuscript support for other ancient documents and books, it becomes extremely clear that no other ancient piece of literature can stand up to the Bible. The average secular work from antiquity survives on only a handful of manuscripts, the New Testament has survived on multiple thousands of manuscripts. There are close to five thousand Greek manuscripts, and an additional thirteen thousand manuscript portions of the New Testament. This does not include the eight thousand copies of the Latin Vulgate and more than one thousand copies of other earlier versions.

Visual Comparison: Other Books of Antiquity vs. New Testament:

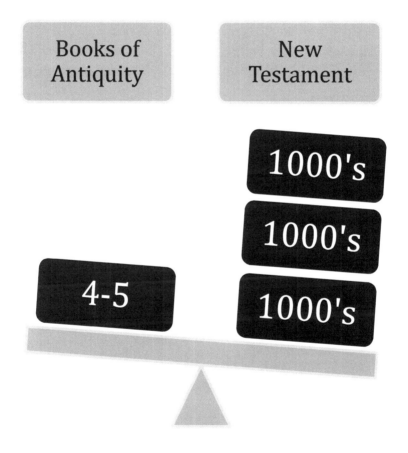

Main Tests of Canonicity

1.) <u>Apostolicity</u> – the test of Apostolicity means that a book must have been written by an Apostle for a close associate of an Apostle.

2.) <u>Rule of Faith</u> – this refers to the conformity of the teachings of the book and the doctrine of the rest of the accepted texts. The document had to be consistent with already established Christian truth. If the document supported heretical teaching it was rejected.

3.) <u>Consensus</u> – this refers to the widespread and continuous use of a document by the churches. The books that were included in the Canon had widespread usage and a consensus of acceptance as Holy Scripture.

The Logical Argument

This argument states that God would protect the gathering of the books into the canon because He had originally written each one. The argument is based on the following premise:

- God had a message He wanted to reveal to man

- God knew His message would be attacked from without

- God knew the recipients of His message were not scholars but were average people in average circumstances

- Therefore, God could be expected to personally guarantee the contents of the canon of Scripture, its accuracy, its compilation process, because by doing so He would assure His message to be transmitted to future generations, complete, without error or corruption and without any additions or deletions to it.

Deuteronomy 4:2 *"Ye shall not add unto the word which I command you, neither shall ye diminish ought from it, that ye may keep the commandments of the LORD your God which I command you."*

Revelation 22:18-19 *"For I testify unto every man that heareth the words of the prophecy of this book, If any man shall add unto these things, God shall add unto him the plagues that are written in this book: And if any man shall take away from the words of the book of this prophecy, God shall take away his part out of the book of life, and out of the holy city, and from the things which are written in this book."*

EARLY CHURCH FATHERS

Polycarp (69-155) was one of the well-known martyrs of the early church, Polycarp identified as a disciple of John the Apostle. What we know of Polycarp comes from his pupil and disciple, Irenaeus (d. 202), apologist and theologian, and later bishop of Lyons, Gaul [France]. Polycarp was one of the last leaders who was won to Christ by an Apostle [John] and knew many who had seen Jesus. *Philip Schaff*, wrote concerning Polycarp's forceful ministry against paganism that he was denounced throughout all Asia Minor as the *"atheist,"* that is, *"the teacher of Asia, the destroyer of our gods."*

[25]He was seen as glorifying a dead man and his messages on the teachings and miracles of Jesus, which John had told him firsthand, were convincing. **Schaff** reports of his letter to the Philippian church, of his focus on Christ saying, "*Of Christ it speaks in high terms as the Lord, who sits at the right hand of God to whom everything in heaven and earth is subject*". [26]

Elliott Wright wrote, "*He was the gentlest...of men...a case study in humility.*" He was remembered as a man of prayer—a man who, according to one ancient source, "*prayed constantly night and day*" – "*prayer that did not interfere with his daylight hours devoted to teaching and his night to studying the Scripture*". When persecution broke out in 156 A.D. every attempt was made to get him to recant his faith in the "cult" of Jesus. "Why, what harm is there in saying, 'Caesar is Lord' and offering incense and saving yourself," the officials continued pleading, "Swear by the divinity of Caesar; repent", but Polycarp did no such thing and instead it is recorded the following took place:

Polycarp is recorded as saying on the day of his death, "*Eighty and six years I have served Him, and He has done me no wrong*". Polycarp goes on to say "*How then can I blaspheme my King and Savior? You threaten me with a fire that burns for a season, and after a little while is quenched; but you are ignorant of the fire of everlasting punishment that is prepared for the wicked.*" Polycarp was burned at

---

[25] Schaff, P. (1979). *Ante-Nicene Christianity, vol. 2 of History of the Christian Church.* Grand Rapids, MI: Eerdmans.
[26] Schaff, P. (1979). *Ante-Nicene Christianity, vol. 2 of History of the Christian Church.* Grand Rapids, MI: Eerdmans.

the stake and was pierced with a spear for refusing to burn incense to the Roman Emperor. On his farewell, he said "*I bless you Father for judging me worthy of this hour, so that in the company of the martyrs I may share the cup of Christ.*"[27]

Clement of Rome - His epistle, 1 Clement (c. 96), was copied and widely read in the Early Church. Clement calls on the Christians of Corinth to maintain harmony and order. It is the earliest Christian epistle aside from the New Testament.

Ignatius of Antioch - Ignatius of Antioch (also known as Theophorus) (c. 35–110) was the third bishop or Patriarch of Antioch and a student of the Apostle John. In route to his martyrdom in Rome, Ignatius wrote a series of letters which have been preserved. Important topics addressed in these letters include ecclesiology, the sacraments, the role of bishops, and the Incarnation of Christ. He is the second after Clement to mention Paul's epistles. [28]

Papias of Hierapolis - Very little is known of Papias apart from what can be inferred from his own writings. He is described as "*an ancient man who was a hearer of John and a companion of Polycarp*" by Polycarp's disciple Irenaeus (c. 180). Eusebius adds that Papias was Bishop of Hierapolis around the time of Ignatius of Antioch. In this office Papias was presumably succeeded by Abercius

---

[27] *Polycarp.* (n.d.). Retrieved 4 10, 2018, from Wikipedia: The Free Encyclopedia: http://en.wikipedia.org/wiki/Polycarp

[28] *Church Fathers.* (n.d.). Retrieved 4 9, 2018, from Wikipedia: The Free Encyclopedia: http://en.wikipedia.org/wiki/Church_Fathers

of Hierapolis. The name Papias was very common in the region, suggesting that he was probably a native of the area. The work of Papias is dated by most modern scholars to about 95–120.[29]

CONCLUSION:

Fundamentalist do not believe in Apostolic succession or that anyone person is ordained of God to be over the whole of the church, like Catholicism does. We do not believe this way because the Bible teaches no such thing. Part of Our Fundamental DNA is acknowledging the sole authority of Scripture over our faith and practice. The promise Christ gave *"… I will build my church; and the gates of hell shall not prevail against it." **Matthew 16:18**,* applies to the church as a whole and not just to Peter or the other Apostles.

The main order and responsibility of the church is the Great Commission. We are responsible to get the Gospel out to a sin filled and dying world. The church has the hope the world needs, the church needs to be sharing that hope. The early church did a good job of evangelizing and sharing the Gospel to their known world. Could the same statement be said about the church of the 21st century?

Early on, heresy and errors were creeping into the church. Some of these were pretty significant and had no basis in Scripture. Jude gave us a warning against false teachers and false teachings in His Epistle. The warning was given 2,000 years ago, but it is still just as applicable today. (***Jude 2-5*** *- Beloved, when I gave all diligence to write*

---

[29] *Church Fathers*. (n.d.). Retrieved 4 9, 2018, from Wikipedia: The Free Encyclopedia: http://en.wikipedia.org/wiki/Church_Fathers

unto you of the common salvation, it was needful for me to write unto you, and exhort you that ye should earnestly contend for the faith which was once delivered unto the saints. For there are certain men crept in unawares, who were before of old ordained to this condemnation, ungodly men, turning the grace of our God into lasciviousness, and denying the only Lord God, and our Lord Jesus Christ. I will therefore put you in remembrance, though ye once knew this, how that the Lord, having saved the people out of the land of Egypt, afterward destroyed them that believed not.)

Dr. Lawrence D. Hufhand commented on this passage in Jude in his booklet *"The Acts of the Apostates"* and said *"We are ordered, compelled, constrained, to "contend for the faith," a faith that was once and forever, delivered to the saints. Faith here means "The full body of truth." In other words, nothing in this Book we call the Bible is to ever be slighted or minimized. It is the complete revelation of God to man and we are to defend it with our logic, as well as our life."*[30]

Polycarp identified as disciple of the Apostle John and that he was won to Christ by the Apostle. It is said of Polycarp that he had a forceful ministry against paganism throughout Asia Minor. It is also reported that though his ministry and preaching style were very forceful, he was a very humble man and gentle in his spirit. He was also a man who was very dedicated to his Savior and worked tirelessly in his ministry to the church and for Christ and was faithful until the end. This is a tremendous example for the church today; the

---

[30] Hufhand, D. L. (2011). *The Acts of the Apostates.* Indianapolis, IN: Lift Ministries.

dedication to Christ and the Great Commission, only if all of us had the same kind of dedication.

Chapter Four Key Fundamental Principles:

1.) <u>Key Fundamental</u> – **Sole Authority of Scripture**. Through this chapter we learned the importance of the absolute authority of Scripture, and standing strong on this key conviction. Tradition should not have any authority over Scripture; church dogma, or dictates should not ever have any authority over Scripture.

2.) <u>Key Fundamental</u> - **A Passion for Winning Souls.** Fundamentalists of the past are noted as having a fervent passion for winning souls. Fundamentalist of the 21st century need to have the goal of being known for having this same kind of passion. Will you make a personal commitment to the Lord to be known as having a passion for winning souls to Him?

PERSECUTIONS OF THE EARLY CHURCH

Acts 5:40-42 "And to him they agreed: and when they had called the apostles, and beaten them, they commanded that they should not speak in the name of Jesus, and let them go. And they departed from the presence of the council, rejoicing that they were counted worthy to suffer shame for his name. And daily in the temple, and in every house, they ceased not to teach and preach Jesus Christ."

J esus Christ was an Israelite, and it might have been expected that the advent of the most illustrious of His race and country, in the character of the Prophet announced by Moses, would have been hailed with enthusiasm by His countrymen. But the result was dramatically different. *"He came unto his own, and his own received him not." John 1:11*. The Jews cried *"Away with him, away with him, crucify him;" John 19:15*, and He suffered the fate of the vilest of criminals. The enmity of the descendants of Abraham to our Lord did not end with His death; they long maintained the bad pre-eminence of being the most severe of the persecutors of His early followers. While the awful events of the trial and crucifixion of

Christ, and the marvels of the day of Pentecost were still fresh in the public mind, their chief priests and elders threw the apostles into prison; and soon afterwards Stephen fell a victim to their misplaced hatred (*Acts 7:54-8:2*). Their infatuation was extreme; and yet it was not unaccountable. They looked, not for a crucified, but for a conquering Messiah. They imagined that the Savior would release them from the bondage of the Roman yoke; that He would make Jerusalem the capital of a prosperous and powerful empire; and that all the ends of the earth would celebrate the glory of His chosen people. Their frustration, in turn, was intense when they discovered that so many of the seed of Jacob acknowledged the son of a carpenter as the Christ and made light of the distinction between Jew and Gentile. In their case, the natural aversion of the heart to a pure and spiritual religion was inflamed by national pride, combined with a heightened bigotry toward Gentiles; and this led to a fervent spirit which was frequently exhibited in their attempts to exterminate the infant Church.

ABBREVIATED TIME LINE

66-70 – Jewish revolt against the Romans. Emperor Titus destroys the Temple in Jerusalem. Jews and Christians flee to all parts of the empire. Antioch becomes the center of Christian activity

71-81 – Roman Colosseum is built. Christians are thrown to wild beasts as entertainment

100 – Approximate death of the Apostle John, the last living of the original twelve disciples

132-135 – Second Jewish rebellion, Jerusalem is destroyed. Most of the population dies or flees

155 – Polycarp, disciple of John the Apostle is burned at the stake. He also referred to the Old and New Testaments as "Scripture"

197 – Christianity sweeps the empire. Tertullian writes "*There is no nation indeed which is not Christian*"

235-270 – Roman persecution of Christians under several Emperors

261 – First actual church buildings erected, prior to this Christians always met in homes

303-304 – Violent persecution of Christians under Diocletian

313 – Edict of Milan, Constantine and Licinius agree to end persecution of Christians

339 – Severe persecution of Christians in Persia (Iran)

367 - Canon of the New Testament slowly collected and confirmed. Books are recognized as authoritative by Althanasius, bishop of Alexandria, in the East, and the Council of Carthage in the West

395-430 – Augustine bishop of Hippo, authors numerous theological works including the City of God. His writing begins to dominate Christendom theology in the West for centuries.

HOSTILITY OF THE ISRAELITES

In almost every town where the missionaries of the cross appeared, the Jews *"opposed themselves and blasphemed;"* and magistrates soon discovered that in no way could they more easily gain the favor of the populace than by inflicting sufferings on the Christians. At about the time of Paul's second visit to Jerusalem after his conversion, Herod, the grandson of Herod the Great, *"killed James, the brother of John, with the sword; and because he saw it pleased the Jews, he proceeded further to take Peter also." **Acts 12:2 - 3.***

The Apostle Peter was delivered by a miracle from his grasp; but it is probable that other individuals of less note, felt the effects of his severity. Even in countries far remote from their native land, the posterity of Abraham were the most bitter and extreme opponents of Christianity. [31]As there was much travel between the land of Israel and Italy, the gospel soon found its way to Rome, the seat of government; and it has been theorized that some civic disturbance created in the great metropolis by the adherents of the traditional Jewish faith, and intended to annoy and intimidate the new sect (Christians), prompted the Emperor Claudius, about A.D. 53, to interfere in the manner described by Luke, and to command *"all Jews to depart from Rome." (**Acts 18:1-2** - After these things Paul departed from Athens, and came to Corinth; And found a certain Jew named Aquila, born in Pontus, lately come from Italy, with his wife Priscilla; (because that Claudius had commanded all Jews to depart from Rome:) and came unto them.)*

The hostility of the Israelites to the followers of Jesus was most formidable in their own country; and for this, as well as other reasons,

---

[31] Killen, W. (1859). *The Ancient Church.* New York, NY

"the brethren which dwelt in Judea" specially required the sympathy of their fellow-believers throughout the Empire. When Paul appeared in the temple at the feast of Pentecost in A.D. 58, the Jews made an attempt on his life; and when the apostle was rescued by the Roman soldiers, a conspiracy was formed for his assassination. Four years afterwards, or about A.D. 62, another apostle, James, who seems to have lived mainly in Jerusalem, finished his ministry by martyrdom.[32]

ROMAN TOLERATION

As the Christians were at first confounded with the Jews, the administrators of the Roman law, for upwards of thirty years after our Lord's death, conceded to them the religious toleration enjoyed by the seed of Abraham. But, from the beginning, *"the sect of the Nazarenes"*, as they were often then referred to, enjoyed very little of the favor of the heathen multitude. Paganism had set its mark upon all the aspects of a person's life and had erected an idol wherever the eye could see. It had a god of War, and a god of Peace; a god of the Sea, and a god of the Wind; a god of the River, and a god of the Fountain; a god of the Field, and a god of the Barn Floor; a god of the Hearth, a god of the Threshold, a god of the Door, and a god of the Hinges. [33] When we consider its power and prevalence in the apostolic age, we need not to wonder at the statement of Paul – *"All that will live godly in Christ Jesus shall suffer persecution."* ***II Timothy 3:12***. Whatever social circle a believer was in or wherever they made an appearance, they were always in some way or form called

---

[32] See Chapter 3 for the account of his death.
[33] Killen, W. (1859). *The Ancient Church*. New York, NY

on to make a protest against this error or that error just in order to remain true to their faith. Because of this, they were assured of being disliked by most people involved in the Pagan idolatry of the day. Also, as a result of all the stands they were forced into taking, the members of the Church were soon regarded by the pagans as a depressed and even mentally unstable people with a hatred to the human race in general.

ROMAN PERSECUTION BEGINS

In A.D. 64, when Rome was set ablaze, many blamed Nero for intentionally setting the city on fire while he was in a fit of rage. Nero soon discovered this provoked the wrath of the Roman citizenry; as a result, he attempted to divert the torrent of public indignation from himself, by blaming the Christians. They were already highly disliked and barely tolerated as the propagators of what was considered "*a pernicious superstition*," and the tyrant Nero, no doubt, believed that the mob of the metropolis of Rome was prepared to believe any report to the discredit of these that belonged to the sect of the Nazarene. But even the pagan historian who records the commencement of this first imperial persecution, and who was deeply prejudiced against the disciples of Christ, bears testimony to the falsehood of the accusation. Nero, says **Tacitus**, "*found wretches who were induced to confess themselves guilty; and, on their evidence, a great multitude of Christians were convicted, not indeed on clear proof of their having set the city on fire, but rather on account of their hatred of the human race. They were put to death amidst insults and derision. Some were covered with the skins of wild beasts, and left to be torn to pieces by dogs; others were nailed to the cross; and some, covered over with flammable matter, were lighted up, when the day* *declined, to serve as torches during the night. The Emperor lent his own gardens for the exhibition. He added the sports of the circus, and assisted in person, sometimes driving a curricle, and occasionally mixing with the rubble in his coachman's dress. At length these proceedings excited a feeling of compassion, as it was evident that the Christians were destroyed, not for the public good, but as a sacrifice to the cruelty of a single individual.*"[34] In the evening, it is reported, that Nero would walk through his gardens that would be illuminated by the burning bodies of Christians.

Some writers have maintained that the persecution under Nero was confined to Rome; but various testimonies concur to prove that it extended to the provinces. Paul seems to contemplate its spread throughout the Empire when he tells the Hebrews that they had *"not yet resisted unto blood striving against sin,"* **Hebrews 12:4**, and when he exhorts them not to forsake the assembling of themselves together as they *"see the day approaching"* **Hebrews 10:25**. Peter also apparently refers to the same circumstance in his letter to the brethren *"scattered throughout Pontus, Galatia, Cappadocia, Asia, and Bithynia,"* when he announces *"the fiery trial"* which was *"to try"* them, *I Peter 4:12,* and when he tells them of judgment beginning *"at the house of God"* *I Peter 4:17.* The persecution by Nero was intense and horrific. Many Christians lost their lives by order of Nero, including the Apostles Paul and Peter.[35] The horror with which his name was so long regarded by members of the Church in all parts of the Empire strongly corroborates the statement that the attack on

---

[34] Killen, W. (1859). *The Ancient Church.* New York, NY
[35] Paul was beheaded, and Peter was crucified by order of Nero according to the ancient historian Eusebeius

the disciples in the capital was only the signal for the commencement of a general persecution.

DESTRUCTION OF JERUSALEM

Nero died A.D. 68, and the war which involved the destruction of Jerusalem and of upwards of a million of the Jews, was already in progress. The holy city fell A.D. 70; and the Mosaic economy, which had been virtually abolished by the death of Christ, now reached its practical termination. At the same period the prophecy of Daniel was literally fulfilled; for "*the sacrifice and the oblation*" were made to cease, **Daniel 9:25-27**, as the demolition of the temple and the dispersion of the priests put an end to the celebration of the Levitical worship. The overthrow of the land of Israel contributed in various ways to the advancement of the Christian cause. Judaism, no longer able to provide for the maintenance of its ritual, was exhibited to the world as a defunct system; its institutions, now more narrowly examined by the spiritual eye, were discovered to be but types of the blessings of a more glorious dispensation; and many believers, who had before adhered to the ceremonial law, discontinued its observances. Christ, forty years before, had predicted the siege and desolation of Jerusalem; and the remarkable verification of a prophecy, delivered at a time when the catastrophe was exceedingly improbable, appears to have induced several to think more favorably of the credentials of the gospel. In another point of view, the ruin of the ancient capital of Judea proved advantageous to the Church. With the subversion of their chief city, the power of the Jewish hierarchy sustained a shock from which it would never fully recover; and the disciples were then partially delivered from the attacks of their most relentless and implacable persecutors.

RENEWED PERSECUTION

After the death of Nero, the Church enjoyed a break from persecution, but when Domitian, in A.D. 81, succeeded to the government, the work of persecution recommenced. Domitian governed the Empire fifteen years, but his persecution of the Christians appears to have been limited to the latter part of his reign. About this time, the Apostle John, *"Who bare record of the word of God, and of the testimony of Jesus Christ" **Revelation 1:2**,* was sent as an exile into Patmos, a small rocky island in the Aegaean Sea not far from the coast of Asia Minor. It is said that he had previously survived unhurt from a cauldron of boiling oil into which he had been plunged into while in Rome by order of the Emperor;[36] but this account, from a writer who lived about a century afterwards is the earliest record of this and has been questioned as authentic.

While Christianity during this time, though facing heavy persecution and disdain, was gradually attracting more and more attention, it was also at the same time nobly demonstrating its power as the great regenerator of society. The religion of pagan Rome could not satisfy the wants of the soul; it could neither improve the heart nor invigorate the intellect; and it was now rapidly losing its hold on the consciences of the people. The high places of idol worship often exercised a most demoralizing influence. The vices of some of its most distinguished professors were notorious; and they enjoyed neither the confidence nor the respect of the mass of the people. But, even under the most unpromising circumstances, it soon appeared that Christianity could accomplish social and spiritual changes of a very

---

[36] Killen, W. (1859). *The Ancient Church.* New York, NY

extraordinary character. The Church of Corinth was perhaps one of the least exemplary of the early Christian communities, and yet it stood upon a moral eminence far above the surrounding population; and, from the roll of its own membership, it could produce cases of conversion to which nothing parallel could be found in the whole history of heathendom.

Paul was able to say to this church *"Be not deceived: neither fornicators, nor idolaters, nor adulterers, nor effeminate, nor abusers of themselves with mankind, Nor thieves, nor covetous, nor drunkards, nor revilers, nor extortioners, shall inherit the kingdom of God. And such were some of you: but ye are washed, but ye are sanctified, but ye are justified in the name of the Lord Jesus, and by the Spirit of our God"* **I Corinthians 6:9-11**. The gospel proved itself sufficient to meet the basest needs of man and the highest aspirations of him too. It revealed to men a Friend in heaven who *"sticketh closer than a brother;"* **Proverbs 18:24**, and it assured him of eternal happiness in the enjoyment of fellowship with God, it imparted to him a peace that passeth all understanding. The Roman people witnessed an awe-inspiring event when they saw the primitive followers of Christ dying for Him in the fires of martyrdom. The pagans did not so value their beliefs; but here was a religion which was accounted *"better than life."* You must think that the flames which illuminated the gardens of Nero supplied some spiritual light to the crowds who were present at the sad scenes; and in the unshakable spirit of the first sufferers, the thoughtful citizen might have recognized a belief in a carpenter's son from Nazareth, was much more than that, and that is was destined to yet shake the very foundations of the world for Christ. (**Acts 17:6** - *And when they found them not, they drew Jason* *and certain brethren unto the rulers of the city, crying, These that have **turned the world upside** down are come hither also*;)

After Domitian, there was no officially sanctioned persecution of Christians, though persecution was still carried on by local governments, and many Christian leaders were put to death, including Ignatious, Polycarp, Justin Martyr, Irenaeus, and Cyprian. [37]

When the Emperor Marcus Aurelius (161-180 A.D.) came to power, he issued a decree that those who would identify Christians to the Roman authorities would then in turn be given their property. As a result of this decree throughout the Roman Empire, Christians were being turned in by their neighbors. Many were beheaded and thousands more were thrown to wild animals to provide entertainment for thousands of spectators who flocked to the Roman amphitheaters. [38] Many Christians were burned, and their ashes were thrown into the wind "to prevent their resurrections", was the reason given by the Romans as to why they took this extra step with their remains.

The worst persecution came under the reign of Diocletian, who devoted the full resources of the military to hunt down and destroy all Christians. It is estimated that millions of Christians died during that period![39] Diocletian's successor, Galerius, condemned this persecution and shortly before the end of his life, ordered the end of it.

---

[37] Dr, P. S. (2011). *The Faithful Baptist Witness.* Cleveland, GA: The Old Paths Publications.

[38] Dr, P. S. (2011). *The Faithful Baptist Witness.* Cleveland, GA: The Old Paths Publications.

[39] Dr, P. S. (2011). *The Faithful Baptist Witness.* Cleveland, GA: The Old Paths Publications.

Galerius was succeeded by Constantine, who officially adopted Christianity as the religion of the empire; though there is no solid evidence he ever became a Christian himself. Constantine began to mix the teachings of Christianity with that of various pagan religions that had significant numbers of followers. Constantine was trying to offer something for everyone, but in reality, this began to hasten the pollution that had already began creeping into the church's doctrines and practice. Also, this practice of mixing some of the teachings and traditions of local pagan religions with that of the church, was adopted by the Catholic church as a standard practice.

SOME OF ROMES REASONS FOR PERSECUTION

The Romans gave several reasons for the persecution. We will briefly examine a few of these objections. In these objections, we will notice some fundamental doctrines and truths the early Christians held to and were persecuted for as result of holding to these fundamental truths. Would we be so willing today to suffer the kind of persecution, these early Christians willingly suffered for their fundamentals of faith, for our own fundamentals of faith?

- The Romans did not understand the concept the early Christians had of the separation of church and state. Rome at this time demanded that all religions be licensed by the Roman government and to accept that Caesar was the final authority in their religion. We see in reality two fundamentals of the faith that this violated: first, it violated the separation of church and state, secondly, it also trampled upon the question of ultimate authority over the church. Which at this time,

Christians for the most part, were still maintaining the independence of the local body of believers and that God and His word were the final and ultimate authorities of their faith and practice. Sadly, not too long after this, a lot of Christian assemblies began to fall in line with a universal (catholic) church stance.

• Christians at this time were also being accused of cannibalism. You may ask how would this accusation come about? - It came from the Roman misunderstanding of the Lord's Supper. The pagan and carnal minds of the Romans caused them to naturally assume that when referencing the eating and drinking in remembrance of the Lords body and blood, that actual eating of flesh and drinking of blood was occurring. This again was sadly an unfortunate foreshadowing of an actual heretical teaching that would creep into the budding universal or catholic church movement and that is the belief in the false doctrine of Transubstantiation.[40]

• Christians also, unbelievably to us, were accused of being atheists. Again, how was this accusation possible? – We must keep in mind the cultural setting and context of this time in history. The Romans were used to worshipping multiple gods and idols they could actually see. They could not see the Christian God, so they mistakenly assumed then the Christians actually worshiped nothing because there was no physical idol to see or to touch. Sadly again, this naturally

---

[40] *Transubstantiation* – is the doctrine in which the Catholic church considers the bread and the wine to become the actual body and blood of Christ after the Priest prays over them.

correlates into the false teachings and practices that crept later into the Catholic church of "Image worship" and "Saint Worship". You can unmistakably see paganism interwoven into the Catholic church. Where at first these Christians were sacrificing their lives in defiance of paganism and for the Lord, then later the establish church started embracing and teaching, the very things early believers left at great peril to their own lives, by the grace of God through their salvation in Christ.

BENEFITS OF THE PERSECUTION

Genesis 50:20 *"But as for you, ye thought evil against me; but God meant it unto good, to bring to pass, as it is this day, to save much people alive."*

It has been noted all throughout church history that some of the greatest times of expansion and growth of Christianity have come while it was under some form of persecution. If you look at the explosion of growth, mission works, evangelization that occurred after the crucifixion of Christ: what prompted the Apostles and other believers to scatter from Jerusalem and go into the uttermost parts of the world? – You would have to say that Persecution was a big factor.

Now look at the Christians of the Roman empire. While they were being persecuted and fearing for their life, would not they think of leaving this area and going someplace safe? This in turn would spread their belief and witness to this new area and spread the gospel. Under mild persecution some would leave and take the good news of the Gospel with them, but under heavy persecution most of them that could leave would leave and spread the Gospel even further and greater.

As a result of the heavy Roman persecution, think of all the remote locations, mountain top villages, faraway lands, that these Christians fled to, then all these places now had devout Christians living with them, testifying of Christ. God only knows of the countless millions that were saved and in Heaven today as a result of this horrific chapter in church history. God took what men meant for evil and used it for good (*Genesis 50:20*), and now countless souls are in Heaven as a result. All those that had their lives taken, and their blood spilt for the name of Christ by the hands of the Romans, were not in vain. God honored their efforts and sacrifice, just as His word says, and used this dark time in church history as an opportunity to shine His light of redemption even farther and greater as a result.

CONSTANTINE

Constantine – also known as Constantine the Great, was born 280 A.D. or sometime shortly after this year. Most sources place his birth year somewhere between 280 and 289. He died May 22nd, 337 near what is now known as Izmit, Turkey. He was the first Roman Emperor to embrace Christianity. Though there is no conclusive historical evidence he ever became one.

In 306, Constantine was proclaimed emperor by the army and after a series of military campaigns, palace intrigue, and a political marriage, he then successfully invaded Italy in 312, defeated his brother-in-law outside of Rome, and officially became the Western Roman Emperor. Then after more alliances, and battles, he defeated the

Eastern Roman Emperor and became the sole emperor of a once again united Roman Empire.

After his victory at Rome (October 27, 312), Constantine, in conjunction with his eastern colleague, published in January 313 a religious edict of toleration, which went beyond the edict of Galerius in 311 and granted full freedom to all existing forms of worship, with special reference to the church buildings and property confiscated in the Diocletian persecution, they were ordered to be restored to their rightful owners. But the spirit of the Roman empire was too absolutistic to abandon the prerogative of supervision of public worship. [41] This Constantinian edict, however, was only a temporary measure of the state, it was a transitional step to a new order of things. It set the stage for the elevation of Christianity, specifically to a Catholic hierarchical form of Christianity, with its exclusiveness as the official state religion, this made it tend toward heretical and schismatic teachings.

Constantine practiced a shrewd religious tolerance in his public affairs and governance. He still had pagans in government positions and allowed pagan worship to continue unless it resulted in public displays of immorality as in the obscene case of Venus worship in Phoenicia or in places specifically sacred to Christians.

Throughout his life, Constantine ascribed his success to his conversion to Christianity and the support of the Christian God.

---

[41] Schaff, P. (1889). *History of the Christian Church Volume 3.* Oak Harbor, WA: Logos Research Systems.

The triumphal arch erected in his honor at Rome after the defeat of Maxentius ascribed the victory to the "inspiration of the Divinity" as well as to Constantine's own genius. Constantine left no doubt that to remove error and to propagate the true religion were both his personal duty and a proper use of the imperial position. His claim to be "bishop of those outside the church" may be construed in this light. Other such pronouncements, expressed in letters to imperial officials and to Christian clergy, demonstrate that Constantine's commitment to Christianity was firmer and less ambiguous than some have suggested.[42] Eusebius confirmed what Constantine himself believed: that he had a special and personal relationship with the Christian God, though based on his belief about baptism this leaves this statement in much doubt.

Constantine had a belief that baptism would cleanse him from all of his sins, and therefore it is reported he put it off until his deathbed, because he did not want to sin afterwards and thereby might lose his sacramental forgiveness of sins and end up going to hell. He had the wrong concept of what salvation was and it is because of this reason that there is no clear testimony of his salvation many doubt he ever became a Christian.

Constantine had strange inconsistencies of religious thoughts and practices, though he did not possess a clear testimony of salvation, and he did not get baptized until his deathbed, he fancied himself a

---

[42] J.F. Mathews, D. M. (2018, August 27). *Constantine - Roman Emperor*. Retrieved from Encyclopedia Britannica: https://www.britannica.com/biography/Constantine-I-Roman-emperor

preacher of the gospel and even declared himself the Bishop of Bishops, he convened the first general council and made Christianity the official religion of the empire, all without a clear testimony of salvation, and before he was baptized.

CONCLUSION:

The early church suffered heavy persecution, yet it flourished and grew rapidly. Times of heavy persecution are often times of great expansion in the church. The Emperor Nero persecuted the early Christians in a devastatingly way, yet they kept living for Christ, they kept evangelizing, they kept growing, they kept doing missionary work. It should not depend on who is in charge of government, we should just keep working and witnessing for Christ. It should not matter the laws they put in place, if those laws violate Scripture we need to follow Scripture. God and His word are the ultimate authority, and because of that *"we ought to obey God rather than man"* **Acts 5:29**.

Nero died A.D. 68, and the war which involved the destruction of Jerusalem and of upwards of a million of the Jews, was already well underway. The holy city fell in A.D. 70; and the Mosaic economy, which had been virtually abolished by the death of Christ, now reached its practical termination. At the same, as stated earlier, the prophecy of Daniel was literally fulfilled; for *"the sacrifice and the oblation"* were made to cease, **Daniel 9:25-27**.

The worst persecution came under the reign of Diocletian who devoted the full resources of the military to hunt down and destroy all Christians. It is estimated that millions of Christians died during that period![43] Diocletian's successor, Galerius, condemned this persecution and shortly before the end of his life ordered the end of it. Galerius was succeeded by Constantine who officially adopted Christianity as the religion of the empire.

In 306, Constantine was proclaimed emperor by the army and after a series of military campaigns, palace intrigue, and a political marriage, he then successfully invaded Italy in 312, defeated his brother-in-law outside of Rome, and officially became the Western Roman Emperor. Then, after more alliances and battles, he defeated the Eastern Roman Emperor and became the sole emperor of a once again united Roman Empire.

Constantine established the state church form of Christianity as the official religion of the empire. His efforts help bring an end to the state sponsored persecution of his time, but his efforts also sowed the seeds of corruption and the universal catholic church sprang forth from these seeds that were sown by Constantine.

Chapter Five Key Fundamental Principles:

1.) <u>Key Fundamental</u> – **Separation of Church and state**. This is a concept the Romans struggled with, but this is fundamental to our belief and practice. We believe there should be no state sponsored church. We believe the local church should be independent of any governing authority, and have

---

[43] Dr, P. S. (2011). *The Faithful Baptist Witness.* Cleveland, GA: The Old Paths Publications.

as its sole authority for faith and practice God and His Holy Word.

2.) <u>Key Fundamental</u> – **Proper understanding and observance of the Lords Super.** When we partake of the Lords Supper, in observance of Him, according to the commandment found in the Scripture to do so, we know and believe that the bread and grape juice only are a representation of the blood and body of Christ, and do not actually become the blood and body of Christ.

3.) <u>Key Fundamental</u> – **No Compromise on the teachings of the Bible.** The early Christians, for the most part, did not compromise their beliefs, or their practice of them, even if it meant losing everything including their lives. We need to be as adamant about not compromising our beliefs and convictions with the world as they were. We need to ask the Lord to help us examine ourselves to see if there are any areas of compromise in our life, and to then help us root out those areas so we may become more like Christ, and thereby more effective witnesses for Him.

REVIEW AND CONCLUDING THOUGHTS

John 1:1-5 *"In the beginning was the Word, and the Word was with God, and the Word was God. The same was in the beginning with God. All things were made by him; and without him was not any thing made that was made. In him was life; and the life was the light of men. And the light shineth in darkness; and the darkness comprehended it not."*

Christ and His Word are the foundation that all our fundamental beliefs and practices are built upon, or they at least should be. We need to be on guard against traditions taking precedence over Scripture. The church is the only place that Christ is the head of, and the place He is directly attached (*Ephesians 1:22-23 - And hath put all things under his feet, and gave him to be the head over all things to the church, Which is his body, the fulness of him that filleth all in all.*) The church is a place to call the elders together to pray for healing (*James 5:14-16*). It is the place you discover your spiritual gifts and use them to serve others. It is the place the Pastor can be found to help minister to broken lives. It is the place where

Christ wants His death to be remembered (*I Corinthians 11:24-26*). The church is the pillar and foundation of truth.

ESSENTIAL OF THE CHURCH

Colossians 1:18 *"And he is the head of the body, the church: who is the beginning, the firstborn from the dead; that in all things he might have the preeminence."*

The number one essential of the church is Christ. Unless Christ is the center of everything in the church, there is no point in doing anything. It can be compared to a person believing in Christ for salvation, but not believing in the resurrection or life after death, what is the point? Not having Christ in the center of all the church does is like being alive but choosing not to have a heart or lungs. You won't be alive very long without them, and a church that neglects to put Christ in the center of all it does won't be alive very long either.

DISCIPLESHIP

II Timothy 2:2 *"And the things that thou hast heard of me among many witnesses, the same commit thou to faithful men, who shall be able to teach others also."*

From the very beginning, discipleship was not only a command, but also an essential component of the church, it was necessary for the proper functioning of the church. Discipleship is how we pass on our fundamental beliefs and practices, it is how we can help train and equip young believers in Christ to go out, and in turn win others, and perpetuate the process from generation to generation. We need to put emphasis on what Christ put emphasis on. Just look at how long He discipled the twelve before leaving them, and sending them out? Look how thorough Christ was in His discipleship. We need to consider these facts and let them challenge us to do all we can to fulfill this needed component of ministry.

SACRIFICIAL MINISTRY

Beginning with the cross and the crucifixion of Christ, the beginnings of the church witnesses a lot of bloodshed. Following the Savior over the next several years, the church endured many martyred heroes of the faith. The church was under hard persecution by Judaism and Paganism. Jesus had spoken to His followers of persecution to come. He made it no secret that following Him, and doing His work would not be the easy road, but that it would require dedication, hard work, and sacrifice. (*John 15:19-20 - If ye were of the world, the world would love his own: but because ye are not of the world, but I have chosen you out of the world, therefore the world hateth you. Remember the word that I said unto you, The servant is not greater than his lord. If they have persecuted me, they will also persecute you; if they have kept my saying, they will keep yours also.*)

Over the centuries since, there have been many, too numerous to count, whose only crime was that of being a Christian. Who were then persecuted, tortured, or put to death because of that belief. These martyrs gave their whole life over to Christ, they laid their all on the altar for Him. Can we say we have this same mindset when it comes to sacrifice and ministry?

ORDINARY MEN

Jesus called his disciples into the ministry, but they generally were not what we would consider ministry ready. They were not polished, not great orators, they did not possess a lot of natural ability to do what they were called to do. But they had one thing going for them; they were called into the ministry by Jesus Christ. If He if calls you, He will equip you with what you need to succeed. Not everyone is called to preach, but everyone is called to minister. God delights in using those people for His ministry which would be the last ones chosen by men for the position. This ensures God gets the glory, and not the man, because it is obvious that man could not and is not doing it though his own abilities. (*I Corinthians 1:26 - For ye see your calling, brethren, how that not many wise men after the flesh, not many mighty, not many noble, are called*)

The Apostles were ordinary men like you and me. They were called by Jesus into his service and ministry. All but one lived their life for Him and His cause. It is because of their zeal, and willingness to give all for Christ, and His work that you and I are here today to learn of Christ, and have the opportunity to be saved. They helped found the Christian church. They proclaimed the word of God with boldness and without compromise, and we should do no less (*Acts 4: 31 - And when they had prayed, the place was shaken where they were assembled together; and they were all filled with the Holy Ghost, and they spake the word of God with boldness.*)

What a foundation that the Apostles help lay for the establishing of the church! We know Christ is the foundation of the church, but the work, the sacrifice, the testimony in life, and in death from Christ's

Apostles is astounding and awe inspiring to consider, and meditate on. They literally gave all for Christ, they gave all for their fellow believers, they gave all for us too! Let's hope that into the Fundamental DNA of every church is woven much of the faithful and zealous DNA of the Apostles.

Fundamentalist do not believe in Apostolic succession. The office of the Apostle ceased to exist with the death of the Apostles. It was to the church that Christ promised continual existence, not to Peter or to the other Apostles. Christ founded the church, He died for the church, He is the foundation of the church, and during His earthly ministry Christ said *"... I will build my church; and the gates of hell shall not prevail against it."* **Matthew 16:18**. Christ then went on and gave them the Great Commission, which tells them what His church is to do *"Go ye therefore, and teach all nations, baptizing them in the name of the Father, and of the Son, and of the Holy Ghost: Teaching them to observe all things whatsoever I have commanded you: and, lo, I am with you alway, even unto the end of the world. Amen."* **Matthew 28:19-20**.

OUR MISSION

Acts 2:8 *"But ye shall receive power, after that the Holy Ghost is come upon you: and ye shall be witnesses unto me both in Jerusalem, and in all Judaea, and in Samaria, and unto the uttermost part of the earth."*

The origin of the church and its mission does not start with man but with the Son of Man, Christ Jesus. His Great Commission was not given to the Apostles as individuals, but to them and the coming church as a whole. The Apostles, and others who heard Him give this Great Commission, were all soon dead, but the Church, the Church has never died, it is as much alive now as it was at its inception by Christ. Yes, the church has been persecuted, the history of the church is awash in the blood of the saints, it survived the Dark Ages, it survived the persecution from the Catholic church, it survived, and it thrived.

The main order and responsibility of the church is the Great Commission. We are responsible to get the Gospel out to a sin filled and dying world. The church has the hope the world needs, the church needs to be sharing that hope. The early church did a good job of evangelizing and sharing the Gospel to their known world. Could the same statement be said about the church of the 21st century?

AUTHORITY OF SCRIPTURE

Through this little book we can see the importance of the absolute authority of Scripture and standing strong on this key conviction. Tradition should not have any authority over Scripture. Church dogma or dictates should not ever have any authority over Scripture. Scripture is to be at the center of the church. A church, and an individual Christian for that matter, should have all their beliefs and practices established on the solid foundation of Scripture and not on traditions of men.

FAITHFULLNESS IN TRIALS

I Peter 1:6-8 "*Wherein ye greatly rejoice, though now for a season, if need be, ye are in heaviness through manifold temptations: That the trial of your faith, being much more precious than of gold that perisheth, though it be tried with fire, might be found unto praise and honour and glory at the appearing of Jesus Christ: Whom having not seen, ye love; in whom, though now ye see himnot, yet believing, ye rejoice with joy unspeakable and full of glory:"*

While Christianity, during the time examined in this book, was facing heavy persecution and disdain, it was also gradually attracting more and more attention, and at the same time nobly demonstrating its power as the great regenerator of society. The religion of pagan Rome could not satisfy the wants of the soul; it could neither improve the heart nor invigorate the intellect; and it was now rapidly losing its hold on the consciences of the people. The high places of idol worship often exercised a most demoralizing influence. The vices of some of its most distinguished professors were notorious; and they enjoyed neither the confidence nor the respect of the mass of the people. But even under the most unpromising circumstances, it soon appeared that Christianity could accomplish social and spiritual changes of a very extraordinary character. The Church of Corinth was perhaps one of the least exemplary of the early Christian communities, and yet it stood upon a moral eminence far above the surrounding population; and from the roll of its own membership, it could produce cases of conversion to which nothing parallel could be found in the whole history of heathendom.

NO COMPROMISE

The early Christians, for the most part, did not compromise their beliefs or their practice of them, even if it meant losing everything, including their lives. We need to be as adamant about not compromising our beliefs and convictions with the world as they were. We need to ask the Lord to help us examine ourselves to see if there are any areas of compromise in our life, and to then help us to root out those areas, so we may become more like Christ, and thereby more effective witnesses for Him.

FOR THE CAUSE OF CHRIST

My prayer and hope is this little book on The Ancient Church and our Fundamental Beliefs has ministered to you, or helped you in some way. I pray we can emulate the convictions, the courage, the work ethic, the dedication, and the willing sacrificial spirit these early Christians possessed in such immense proportions, today as much as they did then. Imagine what can be done for the cause of Christ if we did. Perhaps if all of us took Gods Mission, that was given to the church, as seriously as these early Christians did, we too could be known for turning the world upside down (*Acts 17:6b – These that have turned the world upside down are come hither also.*) Lets us have as our prayer that this statement in *Acts 17:6*, sometime in the future, could be truthfully said about this current generation of Christians as well. That we too "*turned the world upside down*" for the cause of Christ!

Image Credits

Initial picture after title page: **Spencer Collection**, (1500) The New York Public Library. "Full-page miniature of the Apostles in ships on the Sea of Galilee (probably illustrates Mark 4:35-40)" New York Public Library Digital Collections. Accessed October 3, 2018. http://digitalcollections.nypl.org/items/510d47da-ea9c-a3d9-e040-e00a18064a99

Pg. 12: "Ascension of Christ" – **Gustave Gore** (1832 – 1883)

Pg. 14: **Giulio Clovio** (1550) - Manuscripts and Archives Division, The New York Public Library. "Full-page miniature of Pentecost. Elaborate full border with human figures" *The New York Public Library Digital Collections*. 1550. http://digitalcollections.nypl.org/items/510d47da-e654-a3d9-e040-e00a18064a99

Pg. 35: **Lucas Cranach** (1512) - The Miriam and Ira D. Wallach Division of Art, Prints and Photographs: Print Collection, The New York Public Library. "The Martyrdom of St. Peter" New York Public Library Digital Collections. Accessed October 3, 2018. http://digitalcollections.nypl.org/items/c83d2890-fb4c-0133-3f05-00505686a51c

Pg. 40: **Lucas Cranach** (1512) - The Miriam and Ira D. Wallach Division of Art, Prints and Photographs: Print Collection, The New York Public Library. "The Martyrdom of St. Andrew" *The New York Public Library Digital Collections*. 1512. http://digitalcollections.nypl.org/items/c91ed780-fb4c-0133-9e21-00505686a51c

Pg. 55: **Lucas Cranach** (1512) - The Miriam and Ira D. Wallach Division of Art, Prints and Photographs: Print Collection, The New York Public Library. "The Martyrdom of St. Thomas" *The New York Public Library*

Digital Collections. 1512. http://digitalcollec-
tions.nypl.org/items/ccee9ff0-fb4c-0133-76f0-00505686a51c

Pg. 60: **Lucas Cranach** (1512) - The Miriam and Ira D. Wallach Division
of Art, Prints and Photographs: Print Collection, The New York Public Library. "The Martyrdom of St. James Minor" *The New York Public Library
Digital Collections*. 1512. http://digitalcollec-
tions.nypl.org/items/ce4c6a40-fb4c-0133-929b-00505686a51c

Pg. 67 – "Saul's Conversion" – **Gustave Gore** (1832 – 1883)

Pg. 78 – "Paul's Shipwreck" – **Gustave Gore** (1832 – 1883)

Bibliography

Barr, J. (1983). *Holy Scripture, Canon, Authority, Criticism.* Philadelphia, PA: Westminster.

Cannings, P. (2018). *Big Idea Sermons.* Nashville, TN: B & H Publishing Group.

Carroll, J. (1931). *The Trail of Blood.* Challenge Press.

Church Fathers. (n.d.). Retrieved 4 9, 2018, from Wikipedia: The Free Encyclopedia: http://en.wikipedia.org/wiki/Church_Fathers

Cummings, D. G. (2008). *A Study of the Twelve Apostles.* Mustang, OK: Tate Publishing.

Fanning, D. (2018, April 9th). *Missions of the Early Church.* Retrieved from Digital Commons Liberty University.

Hufhand, D. L. (2011). *The Acts of the Apostates.* Indianapolis, IN: Lift Ministries.

J.F. Mathews, D. M. (2018, August 27). *Constantine - Roman Emperor.* Retrieved from Encyclopedia Britannica: https://www.britannica.com/biography/Constantine-I-Roman-emperor

Killen, W. (1859). *The Ancient Church.* New York, NY.

Koine Greek Language. (2018, September 17). Retrieved from Encyclopedia Britannica: https://www.britannica.com/topic/Koine-Greek-language

MacArthur, J. (2002). *Twelve Ordinary Men.* Nashville, TN: Thomas Nelson.

Malone, T. (1989). *The Church.* Murfreesboro, TN: Sword of the Lord Publishers.

Marshall, I. H. (1983). *The Acts of the Apostles.* William B. Eerdmans.

Polycarp. (n.d.). Retrieved 4 10, 2018, from Wikipedia: The Free Encyclopedia: http://en.wikipedia.org/wiki/Polycarp

Ruffin, C. B. (1970). *The Twelve - The Lives of the Apostles After Calvary.* Huntington, IN: Our Sunday Visitor Publishing.

Schaff, P. (1889). *History of the Christian Church Volume 3.* Oak Harbor, WA: Logos Research Systems.

Steele, R. (1995). *Practical Bible Illustrations from Yesterday and Today.* Chattanooga, TN: AMG International, Inc. .

Stringer, P. (2011). *Faithful Baptist Witness.* Cleveland, GA: Old Paths Publications.

Walvoord, J. &. (1989). *The Bible Knowledge Commentary.* Colorado Springs, CO: David C. Cook.

Wiersbe, W. (2007). *The Wiersbe Bible Commentary: New Testament.* Colorado Springs, CO: David C. Cook .